Isaiah

Baker Bible Guides

General Editors:
Ian Coffey and Stephen Gaukroger

Old Testament Editor: Stephan Dray
New Testament Editor: Stephen Motyer

Acts: Stephen Gaukroger
Philippians: Ian Coffey
1 Peter: Andrew Whitman

Isaiah

Free to Suffer and to Serve

Philip Hacking

Baker Books
A Division of Baker Book House Co
Grand Rapids, Michigan 49516

© 1994 by Philip Hacking

Published by Baker Books
a division of Baker Book House Company
P. O. Box 6287, Grand Rapids, MI 49516-6287

First American edition 1995

Printed in the United States of America

First published in 1994 by Crossway Books
Nottingham, England

Library of Congress Cataloging-in-Publication Data

Hacking, Philip.
    Isaiah : free to suffer and to serve / Philip Hacking. —1st
American ed.
        p.   cm. — (Baker Bible guides)
    "First published in 1994 by Crossway Books, Nottingham, England"
—T.p. verso.
    Includes bibliographical references (p.)
    ISBN 0-8010-2057-3 (pbk.)
    1. Bible. O.T. Isaiah—Commentaries. 2. Bible. O.T. Isaiah—Study
and teaching. I. Title. II. Series.
    BS1515.3.H33   1995
    223'.107—dc20   95-16847

To
the people of God
at Christ Church, Fulwood, Sheffield,
whose encouragement and fellowship
constantly inspire me to new opportunities
of Christian service and witness

Contents

Contents

Baker Bible Guides

Meeting together in groups to study the Bible appears to be a booming leisure-time activity in many parts of the world. This series has been designed to help such groups—and, in particular, those who lead them.

We are also aware of the needs of those who preach and teach to larger groups as well as the hard-pressed student, all of whom often look for a commentary that gives a concise summary and lively application of a particular passage.

We have tried to keep three clear aims in our sights:

1. To explain and apply the message of the Bible in non-technical language.
2. To encourage discussion, prayer and action on what the Bible teaches.
3. To enlist authors who are in the business of teaching the Bible to others and are doing it well.

All of us engaged in the project believe that the Bible is the Word of God—given to us in order that people might discover Him and His purposes for our lives. We believe that the 66 books which go to make up the Bible although written by different people, in different places, at different times, through different circumstances, have a single unifying theme: that theme is salvation.

All of us hope that the books in this series will help people get a grip on the message of the Bible. But most important of all, we pray that the Bible will get a grip on you as a result!

Ian Coffey and Stephen Gaukroger

Note to readers

In our Bible Guides we have developed special symbols to make things easier to follow. Every passage therefore has an opening section which is the passage in a nutshell.

The main section is the one that makes sense of the passage.

Questions
Every passage also has special questions for group and personal study after the main section. Some questions are addressed to us as individuals, some speak to us as members of our church or home group, while others concern us as members of God's people worldwide.

Digging deeper
Some passages, however, require an extra amount of explanation, and we have put these sections into two categories. The first kind gives additional background material that helps us to understand something complex. For example, if we dig deeper into the Gospels, it helps us to know who the Pharisees were, so that we can see more easily why they related to Jesus in the way they did. These technical sections are marked with a spade.

Important doctrines
The second kind of background section appears with passages which have important doctrines contained in them, and which we need to study in more depth if we are to grow as Christians. Special sections that explain them to us in greater detail are marked with this symbol.

How to use this book

This book has been written on the assumption that it will be used in one of three ways:

- for individuals using it as an aid to personal study
- for groups wishing to use it as a study guide to Isaiah
- for those preparing to teach others.

The following guidelines will help you to get the most from the material.

Personal study
One of the best methods of Bible study is to read the text through carefully several times, possibly using different versions or translations. Having reflected on the material it is a good discipline to write down your own thoughts before doing anything else. At this stage the introduction of other books can be useful. If you are using this book as your main study resource, then read through the relevant sections carefully, turning up the Bible references that are mentioned. The questions at the end of each chapter are specifically designed to help you to apply the passage to your own situation. You may find it helpful to write your answers to the questions in your notes.

It is a good habit to conclude with prayer, bringing before God the things you have learned. If you follow the chapters of this book as a guide for studying Isaiah you will find it divides up into fifty-eight separate studies of manageable length.

Group study

There are two choices:

a. You can take the twenty-two main sections as weekly studies. These are of unequal length, divided according to the sense of the text, so you may wish to select sections that suit the length of your course.

b. You can opt for a selection of the fifty-eight separate chapters, each featuring three or four study questions.

Members of the group should follow the guidelines set out above for *Personal study*. It is recommended that your own notes should contain:

a. Questions or comments on verses that you wish to discuss with the whole group.

b. Answers to the questions at the end of each section.

The format of your group time will depend on your leader, but it is suggested that the answers to the questions at the end of each section form a starting point for your discussions.

Teaching aid

If you are using this book as an aid to teaching others, note that the book of Isaiah has been divided into twenty-two sections as follows:

Coping with a crisis	1:2–31
God's plans and ours	2:1 – 4:6
Our response to God's love	5:1–30
The call to witness	6:1–13
Storm and sunshine: God acts when we are weakest	7:1 – 9:7
God's anger and our salvation	9:8 – 12:6
Messages for the nations	13:1 – 24:23
God's final victory	25:1 – 27:13
Political crisis: God's help or man's?	28:1 – 31:9
Salvation and its dark prelude	32:1 – 35:10
God tests his servants	36:1 – 39:8
Preparing the way for the Lord	40:1–31
God states his case	41:1 – 42:17
Inconstant servants and unchanging Lord	42:18 – 45:8

The divisions are not all of equal length but break up the text without destroying the flow of the teaching of the book. Each section contains chapters (never more than four per section) which deal with the key points of the text. If twenty-two sessions are too many for your course you can omit some and/or merge some of the shorter ones. The questions at the end of each chapter can easily be adapted for group use.

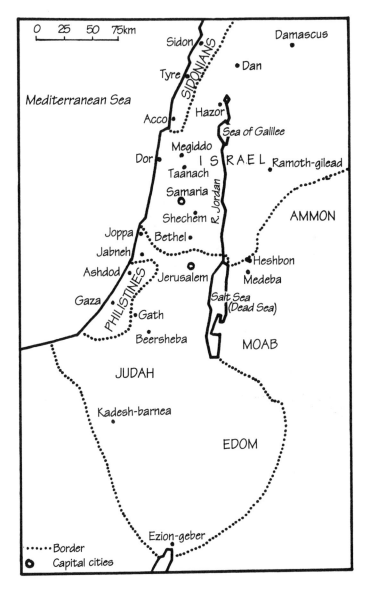

Israel and Judah in the time of Isaiah

Simplified time chart illustrating the Book of Isaiah

Isaiah prophesied for about 60 years (740–700 BC) in the southern kingdom of Judah (see map on previous page). During this time the northern kingdom, Israel, was conquered by the Assyrians and many Israelites were taken into exile (722 BC, see page 50).

Kings of Judah in Isaiah's time:	Uzziah	769–740
	Jotham	740–732
	Ahaz	732–716
	Hezekiah	716–687

Important events happening after Isaiah's death:

612	Fall of Nineveh. Assyrian empire conquered by Babylon.
605	Battle of Carchemish. Daniel and others exiled to Babylon.
587	Jerusalem falls to Babylon (Nebuchadnezzar II). More Jews exiled to Babylon.
539	Babylon falls to Persia under King Cyrus.
538 onwards	– exiles begin to return, to rebuild the walls of Jerusalem (Nehemiah) and the temple (Ezra).
516	Jerusalem temple completed.

Note: all dates are approximate.

Introduction

Isaiah 1:1

Isaiah the royal prophet

I have used the phrase 'the royal prophet' because clearly Isaiah had the ear of kings: he has a confrontation with King Ahaz (7:3); King Hezekiah sends for him in a time of great trouble (37:2); and he was commissioned as a prophet in the year that King Uzziah died (6:1). But not only did Isaiah talk to kings, he actually predicted, more than any other prophet, the Messiah as King. We often think of prophets as those who foretell what is going to happen. Actually most prophets did very little foretelling (they preached to the people of their day) but Isaiah did; the coming of a king is foretold in chapters 7 and 9, a message clearly prophesying the coming of Christ.

Isaiah is also a prophet of royal matters, a prophet who sternly exposes evil and emptiness. He is very much like his contemporaries in the 8th century before Christ. Amos, Hosea and Micah formed a great prophetic combination with Isaiah. In Micah 6:8 appears this classic verse: '... what does the LORD require of you? To act justly and to love mercy and to walk humbly with your God.' To 'act justly' sums up Amos, to 'love mercy' sums up Hosea, and to 'walk humbly with your God' sums up Isaiah.

He is also very much the evangelical prophet who gave us the good news of Christ long before Jesus came to the earth. There is more of the gospel in Isaiah than in any other book of the Old Testament. Indeed he was being true to his name which means 'the Lord saves'. In the opening chapter is the heart of the gospel of salvation: 'Though your sins are like scarlet, they shall be as white as snow' (verse 18). An aspect of the gospel which Isaiah emphasizes is that of the Suffering Servant (Isaiah 53–4). Here is the promise of the one who would come and bear the sins of all. Another hint of the gospel

15

is that there would be a remnant (mentioned for the first time in 1:9 but a theme running through Isaiah). It is the beginning of the idea of the church.

So Isaiah is a royal prophet and an evangelical prophet; he is also a prophet who emphasizes the holiness of God. If you are going to proclaim the gospel effectively you must start with the holiness of God. We do not start with man and his need, we start with God and his holiness, his sovereignty, his grace. Isaiah has a favourite title for God – 'The holy One of Israel' – a description used more frequently in Isaiah than anywhere else in Scripture (see also 2 Kings 19:22; Psalms 71:22; 78:41; 89:18; Jeremiah 50:29; 51:5). This characteristic phrase appears throughout the book as we have it and is a possible hint about its unity (see also below).

Isaiah was also a long-serving prophet: the kings listed in 1:1 span forty years. Unlike Isaiah, Amos had a short ministry during the reign of Uzziah only: he had a great call, went and obeyed, then retired (Amos 1:1). God calls some of his servants to short-term projects and others to the long-term: Isaiah remained faithfully in the Jerusalem which he loved, and he was there with the ears of kings, the royal prophet for a lifetime. The opening verse says that he had a vision, not just occasionally but consistently, 'in the reigns of Uzziah, Jotham, Ahaz and Hezekiah'; his vision recurred over a span of forty years. That vision Isaiah wanted to share with his people and through the wonder of Scripture with us today.

How many Isaiahs?
Many scholars have challenged the claim that Isaiah wrote the entire book which bears his name. Two or three Isaiahs have been suggested with the main division after chapter 39. This claim is based not so much on evidence of language and certainly not on difference of doctrine but sadly because such scholars deny the possibility of predictive prophecy. This is a regular element of Scripture however and of itself does not show that Isaiah could not have written the whole book.

It is clear that the book divides into two main parts; chapters 1–39 deal with events in Isaiah's own day (1:1 – 35:10) with a historical interlude (36:1 – 39:8) and chapters 40–66 look forward to the Babylonian exile and beyond.

Isaiah's is the only name attached to the book and there are many parallels between the two parts. The most telling is the phrase 'The Holy One of Israel' which occurs twelve times in 1–39, fourteen times in 40–66 and only 6 times elsewhere in Scripture. There are close comparisons between 1:2 and 66:24; 1:5–6 and 53:4–5; 5:20 and 40:30; 35:10 and 51:11 and these examples could be multiplied.

An important argument for the unity of the book of Isaiah is that the New Testament refers to the prophet Isaiah as the author of the whole book. Matthew 12:17–21 quotes Isaiah 42:1–4, Romans 10:16 and 20 quotes Isaiah 53:1 and 65:1. Perhaps most tellingly in John 12:38–40 Isaiah is quoted both from the first part (chapter 6:10) and from the second part (chapter 53:1). The traditional view of one Isaiah still stands the test of time.

1
COPING WITH A CRISIS
Isaiah 1:2–31

Isaiah 1:2–31

A rebellious people

Isaiah's listeners were very religious even while rebelling against God. God condemns their sinful behaviour but out of deep compassion offers forgiveness and hope.

 In this opening section of Isaiah's prophecy he records Israel's rebellion against God and its consequences. Their religious worship, of sacrifice and prayer, is utterly meaningless because their hearts are turned away from God.

God condemns Israel's behaviour

Isaiah's message from God to Israel begins on a note of condemnation. Israel, his chosen people, were like his children and he had provided for them as a father does for his children; and as a father he had a unique relationship with them. But his children had turned away from him and rebelled against him (verse 2) (just as the Prodigal Son had turned against his father in Jesus' narrative (Luke 15:11–32)).

Isaiah highlights their sinful behaviour: 'a brood of evildoers ... given to corruption ... forsaken the LORD' (verse 4), 'no soundness' (verse 6), 'hands full of blood' (verse 15), 'evil deeds ... doing wrong' (verse 16), 'murderers' (verse 22), 'rebels, companions to thieves ... love bribes ... do not defend the cause of the fatherless ... widows' (verse 23). No wonder God said 'I will turn my hand against you' (verse 24).

God disciplines his children

Like any father, God must correct his children when they do wrong. There will be punishment, meted out by the foreign armies whom God uses to punish Judah (verse 7) yet God's love will cause him to stop short of full destruction. Isaiah paints a vivid picture of Jerusalem, 'the daughter of Zion', still surviving in the midst of devastation (verse 8).

God does not want empty religious offerings (verses 10–17)

It hurt to be compared with the cities of Sodom and Gomorrah, totally destroyed by God because of their wickedness (Gen. 18–19), because Jerusalem was full of religious activity. Here is a great prophetic word condemning religious ritual without inner spiritual life, a point also made by Amos (Amos 5:21–24). Religious ritual is not condemned as such but the wrong spirit within it makes God sick. Praying hands will not be seen if they are dirty, bloodstained hands. So God brings a note of command with the rapid imperatives of verses 16–17. It is a call back to the living God and his standards.

Hope for the repentant   (verses 18–31)

The Lord calls on Israel to 'reason together' with him about their situation (verse 18). Despite their sinfulness he offers forgiveness and reconciliation: 'Though your sins are like scarlet, they shall be as white as snow ... if you are willing and obedient ...' (verses 18–19). If they 'resist and rebel' they will face God's judgment (verse 20) but the purpose of his judgment is not to destroy but to purify and restore them. There is the assurance of complete cleansing, foretelling the final demonstration of salvation through Jesus (Revelation 7:14). Here too is the hope of a new Jerusalem, a restored 'City of Righteousness' (verse 26). Isaiah's message to Israel is just as relevant for us today – real repentance brings forgiveness and reconciliation with God through his Son (cf. 1 John 1:9).

Questions

1. How important is the use of the mind in Scripture? Link verse 3 with verse 18 and the complaint of meaningless offerings in verse 13.
2. A church must have some kind of ritual. In what ways may your church be guilty of an empty religion? How can you change it?
3. In the contrasting responses of verses 18–20 where do you find yourself? What is your motivation to share the gospel with others?

2

GOD'S PLANS AND OURS
Isaiah 2:1 – 4:6

Isaiah 2:1–22

A tale of two cities, part 1

Isaiah loves his native Jerusalem. **He has a vision of the city as God means it to be, then a grim realization of the city as it actually is.**

Here Isaiah portrays two pictures of Jerusalem: first as God planned it to be, a beacon in a dark world when 'all nations will stream to it' and turn to God (verses 1–5); and then the reality of a nation who has turned from God to worship idols 'and clasp hands with pagans' (verses 6–9). Finally, Isaiah shows the power and judgment of God (verses 10–22).

God's plan for his people   (verses 2–5)

God meant Jerusalem to be a missionary city, choosing his people to share the light of his word with others. People should be drawn by the truth, and not dragooned into it. They will be drawn not by the beauty of the temple nor by the glory of the ritual but by God's uncompromising truth. Only when the truth of God is shared will there be unity and peace (verse 4). The reverse side of the picture is given in Joel 3:9–10 describing the final days of world conflict. The prophecies in these verses will only be completely fulfilled when Christ returns but already they can be seen in part in the life of the Christian community worldwide. The prophet calls us not to live a life of fantasy, but a life of practical action: 'Come, O house of Jacob, let us walk in the light of the Lord'. In the New Testament John, too, encourages us to 'walk in the light, as he is in the light' (1 John 1:7).

God's plan spoilt   (verses 6–9)

Instead of what the city was intended to be like, the harsh reality was that Jerusalem had been abandoned by God and was dominated by astrology and the occult (verse 6). Instead of Jerusalem feeding the world it was being fed by every kind of false religion, as so often happens with the compromising church in every age. Along with superstition went worldly alliances and materialism (verses 7–8). Jerusalem should have been a demonstration of God's own work: instead it was a man-made mess.

God's final response   (verses 10–22)

Isaiah repeats the phrase 'in that day' (verses 11, 17, 20) as he repeats the refrain 'the splendour of his majesty' (verses 10, 19, 21). There will be a day when God alone is exalted. All man's arrogance will be brought low and all his security will go, including his material resources, his great achievements of commerce and technology, not least his man-made religion. We are foolish to put our trust in anything less than the unchanging God. He will have the last word and there will be no hiding place on that day. Revelation 6:15–17 paints the vivid picture of everyone, from the highest to the humblest, seeking to hide from the 'wrath of the Lamb'. So the prophet urges his fellow citizens to stop trusting in themselves (verse 22), the implication being to trust in God. Only one man can be trusted, Christ himself, and he was to be rejected by his fellow men.

Questions
1. The world looks for universal peace. What recipe for peace can be found in these verses?
2. What are the marks of man-made religion? Think of some contemporary equivalents.
3. Could you be guilty of putting your trust in men and women rather than in God or in Christ?

 Parallels with Micah
The opening verses of this chapter are almost identical to Micah 4:1–3. It is quite possible that the two contemporaries shared this vision, that one picked up the theme and hope from the other

or that God gave them the same message. There is a great unity in the prophetic message.

The Day of the LORD

The phrase, 'In that day', occurs seven times in chapters 2–4. The Old Testament portrays a vision of the Day of the Lord which was seen by optimistic Jews as the day of final victory over all their enemies, but the prophets would remind their listeners that it would be, in fact, a day of purging and judgment. The same theme is seen in the New Testament where 'that day' is seen as the final day of our Lord's return with triumph and also judgment (for example Luke 10:12; 1 Thessalonians 5:4; 2 Timothy 1:18).

Isaiah 3:1 – 4:6

A city rises from the ashes

The prophet denounces injustice and emptiness, then paints a beautiful picture of a society restored.

 Isaiah continues with his list of punishments which will fall on Jerusalem and Judea. All their leaders, their props, will be removed and the only leaders left will be children. Oppression and evil against each other will increase.

Solemn judgment

Isaiah condemns two groups of people here. First he condemns the leaders who have led their people astray (verse 12) and have exploited the poor and vulnerable people, stealing from those who already have very little (verses 14–15). Secondly, he condemns the women of Jerusalem for their pride and materialism. While many suffer from poverty, these women are concerned only with the accumulation of wealth and the public display of their materialism.

Soon their worldly lives will collapse and the poverty which will come on these people is seen as a sign of God's judgment. Those who paraded their wealth with pride will suffer the shame of being treated like cattle in captivity (verse 24). The lovely city will be decimated by war and the men killed in the fighting. The proud women will be left with few men to admire them and will fight over the few who are left. In Jewish society women who were unable to find a husband were objects of shame; now these proud women faced lives of disgrace (4:24 – 5:1).

Isaiah's words are just as relevant in our own society with its emphasis on accumulating wealth and materialistic values. As Christians, we need to re-examine our own attitudes and lifestyles, our concern for the poor and suffering.

27

Spiritual neglect

Judgment in Scripture does not only occur in the future: God can mete out punishment now (see, for example, Romans 1:18). Here he removes not only food and water supplies but all those in positions of leadership and authority so that all support is taken away (verses 1–3). Only children are left to fill the governing roles and the result is anarchy and greater exploitation of the weak (verses 4–7). Irretrievable ruin was the inevitable consequence. God cannot be mocked: to defy his laws ultimately brings disaster and eventually our sins do find us out.

In part, sin brings its own immediate judgment but there will be a final day when God will judge our actions (verses 13–14), not least our attitude and response to the poor and needy (verse 15). These verses are a foretaste of Jesus' challenge to our attitude to the poor (Matthew 25) and are equally applicable to our lives today.

A saved nucleus (4:2–6)

Isaiah looks for two things in the future, a restored city, and God's servant or saviour. The two are linked together. Here Messiah is seen as 'the Branch' (see 11:1). Jesus will be the bearer of fruit for his people in a desolate place. Isaiah introduces the theme of the gospel of individual salvation within the body of God's people and gives a glimpse into the biblical picture of God's book of life (verse 3). Those within that book are not there by merit but by God's cleansing fire. It is reminiscent of a second exodus, a great theme in Isaiah. Cloud, fire and shelter (verses 5–6) remind us of Moses' day. Here again is the picture of the presence of God with his people (see Exodus 13:21–22), foreshadowing the New Testament vision of the church as a temple of the Holy Spirit.

Questions
1. Does the description of luxury in Jerusalem apply to our Western culture today? How can we help society to see its danger?
2. Much of the failure of Jerusalem was the failure of leadership. How can we ensure that this does not happen in the leadership of our church?
3. In the attack on luxury what is God saying to you about your lifestyle?

3

OUR RESPONSE TO GOD'S LOVE
Isaiah 5:1–30

Isaiah 5:1–30

Love song turned lament

The parable of the vineyard. God plants his people but they are unfruitful.

This poignant chapter is a stirring climax to Isaiah's long overture before he describes his call to meet the needs of the world around him.

Love's sorrowful song   (verses 1–7)

This sad song has parallels with Jesus weeping over his Jerusalem (Matthew 23:37–39; Luke 13:34–35). The picture of Israel as God's vineyard is found elsewhere in Scripture (for example Psalm 80:8–16) and is taken up by Jesus (John 15). God has prepared and cared for his vineyard. This reminds us that he has prepared the whole of creation (see Genesis 1–2) but especially he has cared for his own people. So he looks for fruit from his labours but is sadly disappointed (verse 2). 'Fruit' means that he expects righteousness and justice but with Isaiah's Jerusalem the reverse is found. The gap between expectation and reality brings a cry of despair and even a message of rejection. Jesus used the same theme to demonstrate how God had to reject the Jewish people because they had turned their back on him (see Luke 13:6–9).

Love's searching sight   (verses 8–23)

Isaiah records six 'Woes' which represent the bad grapes found by God in his vineyard. The word 'woe' does not mean condemnation so much as sorrow.

1. The exploiters are pinpointed in verses 8–10. The property laws of the Old Testament are important and greed is regularly condemned by the prophets. At the heart of biblical faith there is always social concern.

2. Playboys and pleasure-seekers are exposed, those who care only for pleasure and refuse to face facts (verses 11–17). Amos uses similar words of condemnation (Amos 6:1–7). Mindless escapism is a tragic and common reaction to grim reality. But God will have the last word.

3. The scoffers are condemned with four 'woes' (verses 18–23). They are bold in their blasphemy and mimic the prophet (see 28:7–15). Their topsy-turvy morality (verse 20) foreshadows our Lord's definition of the sin against the Holy Spirit (Matthew 12:31–32). The ultimate blasphemy is to call good evil and evil good.

Love's straight speaking   (verses 24–30)

There is the inevitable judgment upon sin which pays its own wages well (see Romans 6:23). The folly of going against God's laws and spurning God's Word is demonstrated in verse 24: we reject the maker's instructions at our peril. But the active wrath of God is also promised. Here we have a foretaste of Isaiah's teaching of God using foreign nations to bring his own people to their knees in repentance, a theme of Scripture. Even in the darkest days God is in control.

Questions
1. If God can speak through international events what may he be saying to the church of today through the current affairs of men and nations?
2. Consider the six woes and God's condemnation of certain ways of life. Are we guilty in any of these areas?
3. The prophet's chastisement always comes from a loving concern. How can you show love without compromising the truth to those who turn their back on God's ways?

4

THE CALL TO WITNESS
Isaiah 6:1–13

Isaiah 6:1–13
'Here am I. Send me!'

We are given a flashback to the beginning of Isaiah's ministry.

Isaiah recounts here how he was called by God to the ministry of prophecy. He begins with a powerful description of the majesty of the Lord, enthroned 'high and exalted', and his holiness, 'Holy, holy, holy is the LORD Almighty.' Despite his power and holiness he seeks to use ordinary people to fulfil his work.

God's call   (verses 1–4)

The year is clearly marked as 740 BC, the year of King Uzziah's death. But for Isaiah it was more than a date on a calendar. It was a year of tragedy marked by the downfall of Uzziah, once a great king and the hero of the young Isaiah. But when he became powerful Uzziah forgot God, disobeyed his clear instructions, and was afflicted with leprosy. His sad story is recorded in 2 Chronicles 26:16–21 and is a story that has often been repeated in history.

Isaiah had a vision in which he saw God seated on a throne in all his power and majesty. The implication is that whoever occupied the throne of Judah God never changes and *always* occupies his throne. There is never an interregnum in heaven. The temple Isaiah saw (verse 1) is a vision of the temple of God and the whole message is one of majesty and holiness, conveyed by heavenly beings, far above our knowledge but swift to serve. In the Bible holiness and service always go together.

The threefold repetition of the word 'holy' by the seraphim (verse 3) probably has no hint of the Trinity but emphasizes the infinite 'otherness' of God. The message of the seraphim should not be limited to a building like the temple, nor even just to the

Jewish people, but it was appropriate to the whole world. Yet it has a special significance here at the heart of worship in Jerusalem. In verse 4 there is an echo of what happened when Moses met God at Mount Sinai (Exodus 19:18–19, 23) and also a foreshadowing of what happened in Acts 4 when the early disciples prayed, the Holy Spirit came on them and the room shook. It speaks of the power of God displayed when his holiness meets earth's sin.

Isaiah's confession   (verses 5–7)

Any encounter with God should lead to an awareness of our uncleanness. In the New Testament, when Jesus performed the remarkable miracle of bringing in the great catch of fish, Peter asked the Lord to leave him because he was so conscious of his own unworthiness (Luke 5:1–11). Isaiah was made aware not only of the sins of the nation he represented but of his own sin. The sinfulness was not only in Uzziah. There will be no power to preach until the preacher is penitent and leaders in the church today need to remember Isaiah's need for repentance and cleansing before he could minister God's word to Israel.

Then comes the wonderful act of atonement without any intermediaries (in the Old Testament times atonement was usually only obtained through the sacrifice of an animal by the priest [Leviticus 6: 24–27]). There is a real anticipation here of the gospel message of complete forgiveness through Christ where there is penitence. Isaiah's lips were touched as a sign of cleansing and atonement as were Jeremiah's (Jeremiah 1:9) because by them the message would be preached. Ultimately all of us need cleansed lips; the effective Christian must first be the cleansed Christian.

God's commission   (verses 8–13)

God's call to Isaiah came in the form of a question (verse 8), a reminder that he commissions people in different ways. Isaiah was not forced to accept the commission: he had the privilege of choice. God always wants willing volunteers, not forced conscripts. The response of the prophet is a marvellous blend of humility and a desire to serve. Isaiah makes his mark for God, ready for anything. We are reminded of the response of Saul of Tarsus on the Damascus Road (Acts 9, especially verse 20).

But the call to go and tell can be costly. Here is a warning of a double-edged sword which Isaiah would need to remember. It was demonstrated in the ministry of Jesus and the experience of the response to his teaching. There is no avoiding the double effect of the gospel. The same sun which melts also hardens (Malachi 4:1–2). There is no message to bring conversion which will not also bring condemnation. Naturally Isaiah cries ' . . . how long?' The answer is not precise but contains the promise that a remnant will never die out (see 1:9). It will be a lifetime's service, not a short-term excitement. Isaiah is called only to be faithful and to leave success to God.

Questions
1. Consider the parallels with the Damascus Road experience of Paul in Acts 9, and reflect on the consistency of Scripture.
2. 'The whole earth is full of his glory'. Why do you think the whole earth cannot see it?
3. The experience here is a very personal one. At what point should you be saying to the Lord 'Here am I. Send me'? What costs can you foresee?

Isaiah and the New Testament

Isaiah 6 is a much-quoted chapter in the New Testament. John, for example, interprets the glory of God which Isaiah saw as the glory of Jesus (John 12:41). There is in this sense, therefore, no distinction within the godhead. The picture of the robe of God filling the temple (verse 1) is also echoed in Revelation 1:13 in the picture of the glorified Jesus.

But mostly it is verses 9 and 10 which are quoted, in the first six books of the New Testament. In the first three gospels these verses are quoted in the explanation of the parable of the sower and soils which shows the many different responses to the good news preached by Jesus (Matthew 13:1–23; Mark 4:2–20; Luke 8:1–15). John also quotes them in relation to the different responses without recounting the parable (John 12:37–41). In Acts 28:25–28 Paul quotes the same passage to the Jewish leaders who were divided in their opinion of his message of Christ. He used these verses and Isaiah 29:10 in his letter to the Romans (11:8) to explain the hardness in many of his beloved Jewish people.

It has been suggested that the good news of God's kingdom has the effect of melting the hearts of those who are willing to accept it. But those who set themselves against the good news are actually hardened by it. Not only does it not make sense to them but it confirms them in their rebellion.

5

STORM AND SUNSHINE: GOD ACTS WHEN WE ARE WEAKEST
Isaiah 7:1 – 9:7

Isaiah 7:1–25

God promises to come himself

The promise of a virgin birth and the name Immanuel are earthed in a confrontation with the weak King Ahaz in 735 BC.

 Following the glorious vision of God's awesome majesty and power we are brought down to earth in the account of the petty squabblings of neighbouring nations. Ahaz was the grandson of Uzziah: his father Jotham reigned for sixteen years and Isaiah recorded nothing during this time. (The events recorded in this chapter occur at least sixteen years after those in the previous chapter.) Ahaz, unlike his father, 'did not do what was right in the eyes of the LORD his God' (2 Kings 16:2).

Fear is dissolved by faith   (verses 1–9)

Politics are often complex, and foolish mistakes are often made through panic measures. Ahaz was threatened by a coalition between Israel (Ephraim) and Syria (Aram) so he planned an alliance with the enemy, Assyria, to save his skin against attack. (For an account of this event read 2 Kings 16.) Isaiah was told by the Lord to bolster the courage of his fearful king. He took his son Shear-Jashub (a living 'visual aid' with his significant name meaning 'a remnant will return') to meet Ahaz and he promised that trust in God would bring deliverance (verses 7–8).

Man's extremity can become God's opportunity. If we admit our helplessness, God can act. Always in Scripture faith is seen as an antidote to fear (for example, see 28:16). Jesus himself repeated the phrase 'Don't be afraid; just believe' (Mark 5:36). But faith is not leaping or whistling in the dark. It is based on reality. Isaiah points out some home truths about Ahaz's enemies and gives a prediction of their downfall in verses 6–8. Faith demands a firm stand and then God will give signs to help.

God's answer is a child (verses 10–25)

True signs demand faith. Unfortunately Ahaz preferred the world of political realism. Behind the pious language of verse 12 is an unwillingness to accept God's offer. Ahaz already has his own plans but his political alliance will backfire in the Assyrian invasion of Judah (verse 17).

Yet in that context of gloom and rebellion come the great words of hope which are still relevant today. Ahaz will bring in an army but God offers a child (verse 14). This came to fulfilment only in Jesus, as Matthew records (Matthew 1:22–23). Only then was there a king with the true name of Immanuel, God with us. Only then does this promise to Israel have its real fulfilment, not any child, born to any young woman, but the son of God himself entering the world through the obedience of Mary. In the Hebrew language the word translated as virgin describes a young woman of marriageable age; it can also mean in its fuller sense a virgin and so, with hindsight, we can apply it to the birth of Jesus. But equally it can have an immediate fulfilment and this is certainly assumed in these verses. The short-term problem of invasion will have occurred long before this child to be born has come of age (verse 16). By that time the land will be devastated and covered with 'briers and thorns'. There will only be goat's yogurt and honey to eat (verses 22–23). All will be the fault of an unbelieving worldly king.

Yet God will be at work. The prophet can see beyond the immediate disaster to the day of Immanuel. Sadly his own day would first have to know the grim humiliation recorded in verses 18–25 before it would come to its senses and turn back to God.

Questions
1. Can you find parallels in current international affairs? What are they doing about it? What would Isaiah suggest as our response?
2. Does the virgin birth of Christ matter to your church? How can we explain it to enquirers?
3. Immanuel means 'God with us'. Think back over the last week. How has God been with you?

The significance of names in the Bible

In Hebrew days the names of people were very significant and were frequently used to convey a message, hence the play on names in different parts of Scripture. Abram (meaning 'exalted father') would change his name to Abraham, 'father of many' and Sarai to Sarah, 'Princess' (Genesis 17:5–15). In the New Testament Simon would be given the new name Peter ('a rock': Matthew 16:18). Hosea is commanded by God to give his children special names which will convey specific messages to Israel and Judah that they no longer have God's favour (Hosea 1:6, 9). Likewise the two children of Isaiah had names which spoke their own message. The name Shear-Jashub conveys the message that 'a remnant will return', that is, the house of Israel will never be totally destroyed but a portion will always survive and one day return to Israel. The second son of Isaiah was given the name of Maher-Shalal-Hash-Baz (8:3) which speaks of plunder coming quickly and spoil being taken swiftly, a note of impending judgment.

Plays on words

The Hebrew prophets were very skilful in their use of words and sometimes would get a message across by a clever use of words which sounded similar but had different meanings (homonyms). This is seen in Jeremiah 1:11–12 where the word for almond tree is similar to the word which means watching. Through this play on words the Lord draws out a message to and through Jeremiah which is not obvious in the English translation. Here in 7:9b Isaiah uses the same Hebrew verb to emphasize the importance of standing firm in the faith as he uses to describe whether he would stand at all. Various translations have been suggested to convey in English the same play on words. The second half of verse 9 can be translated 'Unsure in your faith, insecure in your life', or 'Hold God in doubt, you'll not hold out'.

The virgin birth

This is a traditional Christian doctrine that Jesus had no human father, but his Father was God. It is based on the very clear teaching of Luke 1:34, written by a doctor, and Matthew 1:18–25. It is probably assumed elsewhere in the New Testament, as in Mark 6:3 where Jesus is called 'Mary's son'. It could well be echoed in the sarcastic emphatic 'we' in John 8:41 where the opponents of Jesus claimed that they were not illegitimate children, with its implied suggestion that Jesus was, because of his unusual birth. It fits well with Paul's phrase in Galatians 4:4 where Jesus is seen as 'born of a woman'.

The doctrine of the virgin birth fits beautifully with the truth of the incarnation with Jesus as the perfect God-man. His parents were both divine and human, thus combining the two natures. Matthew 1:23 quotes Isaiah 7:14 and sees the Virgin Mary as foreshadowed in that verse, which also gives fuller meaning to the title 'Immanuel', 'God with us', in Isaiah. In that way an Old Testament promise has a richer meaning in the light of New Testament truth.

Isaiah 8:1 – 9:7

Light and shadow

The promise of God's child in chapter 9:6–7 is seen against the backcloth of grim religious darkness.

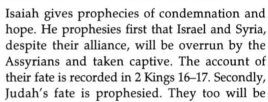

Isaiah gives prophecies of condemnation and hope. He prophesies first that Israel and Syria, despite their alliance, will be overrun by the Assyrians and taken captive. The account of their fate is recorded in 2 Kings 16–17. Secondly, Judah's fate is prophesied. They too will be overwhelmed by the Assyrians but 'reaching only up to its neck' (verse 8), in other words they will not be totally destroyed (see 2 Kings 16 and 18–19).

God's plan and ours   (8:1–10)

When Isaiah's second child is born his name brings the promise of a quick deliverance from the northern kingdoms of Syria (Damascus) and Israel (Samaria) through the intervention of Assyria, which Ahaz feared so much. But there would be a greater foe to fear in Assyria, his former ally. Isaiah contrasts the gentle flow of the river Shiloah, speaking of God's ways, with the mighty flood of the river Euphrates. God will play his people at their own game and bring in Assyrian might to humble them. But the flood will only reach up to the neck (verse 8); there will be a limit to the power of evil. Immanuel's land will be devastated but Jerusalem will survive and the true meaning of Immanuel will remain, that is, 'God with us'. It reminds us of the final promise of Jesus in Matthew's Gospel, following the great commission to go and make disciples: 'I am with you always, to the very end of the age' (Matthew 28:20).

Refuge and ruin   (verses 11–18)

These verses are quoted by Peter in his letter (1 Peter 2:6–8). God is seen as both the foundation stone and a stumbling block. Paul says that the message of the cross is a stumbling block to both Jews and Gentiles (1 Corinthians 1:23). For those who accept Jesus' sacrifice for them, it is the means of salvation. Those who reject him are condemning themselves.

Isaiah needed God's strong hand (verse 11) because his honest words could be seen as treasonable, as did Jeremiah's (Jeremiah 37:13–14). But God commanded Isaiah not to be afraid of what men thought but rather to fear God. 'He is the one you are to fear' (verse 3). If we fear God we will not be afraid of men (see Jesus' words in Luke 12:4–5). The story is told of Bishop Latimer, in the reign of Henry VIII, speaking some stirring words to the king. He almost withheld the challenge because he remembered he was in the presence of the king, until he heard a voice speaking to him clearly that he should remember that he was in the presence of the King of kings. Having heard that, Latimer spoke his message courageously.

Because the majority reject God's Word it is most important for the truth to be preserved (verse 16) so that future generations might hear it. The truth is also preserved in people. Isaiah's disciples may be seen as a foreshadowing of Christ's church. The writer to the Hebrews quotes verse 18 in the context of Jesus and those who follow him (Hebrews 2:13). The church will become God's sign in the world since ultimately God's plan must prevail.

Darkness and dawn   (8:19 – 9:7)

Suddenly the light of verse 18, 'the signs and symbols ... from the LORD Almighty', becomes the groping darkness of verse 19. Now mediums take the place of prophets, calling on the dead on behalf of the living. But the dead cannot help the living, as King Saul discovered when he went to the witch of Endor in his darkness and despair instead of seeking God's help (1 Samuel 28; see also Jesus' parable on the rich man and Lazarus in Luke 16:19–31). We are called always to go back to God's Word: only here is light. Where people will not hear God's Word they would not believe even if someone came back from the dead.

As a result of the people of Israel turning away from God's light 'they will be thrust into utter darkness', which will be broken only

45

by the Messiah. Chapter 9: verses 2–7 contains a beautiful prophecy of the coming of the Messiah to earth to shatter that darkness and bring 'a great light' (verse 2). Seven hundred years before the birth of Christ Isaiah accurately predicts that Galilee, in the northern part of the divided kingdoms of Israel and Judah at this time, will be honoured by the presence of the light of the world. Matthew mentions several times that Jesus came from Galilee (Matthew 2:22; 3:13; 4:12) and specifically links Jesus to Isaiah's prophecy (Matthew 4: 13–16), to confirm his claim to be the Messiah.

Questions

1. Think through the various New Testament links with this passage and see how all Scripture points towards Jesus.
2. In what sense is Jesus a stumbling block in the world? Should Christians sometimes get in the way of authority? How far?
3. Where are you afraid in your witness and how do these verses help you to overcome your fear?

The waters of Shiloah

The source of the waters of Shiloah was to the east of Jerusalem from where it flowed through an aqueduct (Isaiah 7:3) into the Pool of Siloam (an alternative spelling for Shiloah). Nehemiah states that the Pool of Siloam was situated by the King's Garden close to the city walls which he repaired (Nehemiah 3:15). A constant, reliable source of water for the city of Jerusalem would have been vital for the sustenance of its inhabitants. During Hezekiah's reign when the city was besieged by the Assyrians, Hezekiah built a tunnel to protect the water supply (2 Kings 20:20).

The waters of Shiloah are used here by Isaiah to symbolize the gracious, steady and sustaining power of the Lord. They contrast with the mighty river Euphrates (situated in present-day Iraq) which in times of flood overruns its banks and destroys everything in its path.

John records in his gospel the story of the healing of the blind man by Jesus whom he sends to wash his eyes in the Pool of Siloam. Again it is symbolic of God's healing touch. John points out that Siloam means 'Sent'. Could this also be symbolic of Jesus being the 'sent one' or Messiah?

6

GOD'S ANGER AND OUR SALVATION
Isaiah 9:8 – 12:6

Isaiah 9:8 – 10:4

What makes God angry?

God's anger against the arrogance of Israel and its consequences.

Anger is not always condemned in Scripture: Isaiah records the anger of God four times in this section (9:12, 17, 21; 10:4). Like a punishing parent his hand is poised to strike but in chastening love. Isaiah describes it as 'the wrath of the LORD Almighty' (verse 19). God's wrath does not wait for the final day of judgment but is already at work where people disobey him (Romans 1:18) and one day the 'wrath of the Lamb' (Revelation 6:16), a vivid contradiction of images, will be seen, not the fury of someone who has lost his temper but the controlled, loving, hostility to all sin.

The force of God's anger

Judgment is often self-inflicted, for example, the fall of Samaria in the northern kingdom of Israel in 722 BC was as a result of their aggression (verse 9). But God is still involved. God's judgment will move south to Judah (10:1–4).

There is an infectious evil which spreads dangerously like a rotten apple in a box. Punishment which is self-inflicted spreads like a forest fire (verse 18). But God will choose his weapons of judgment: the nation of Assyria is described as 'the rod of my anger' (10:5). Judah's rulers had made a foolish mistake in their political manoeuvring and had turned their backs on God but God was still on his throne and in control of all that was happening (compare Amos 3:7–8). Where people of all walks of life are impenitent (verse 13) God will have to act in judgment (verse 14).

The fruit of man's failure

Isaiah describes the attitude of the Israelites ('Ephraim and the inhabitants of Samaria': verse 9) as one of pride and arrogance: whatever happens to their kingdom they will rebuild it in their own strength and abilities (verse 10). They are rejecting God and denying their need of him – a receipe for disaster – so God will take action against their arrogance.

In the hour of need men do not easily or quickly repent (cf. Revelation 16:11). In the story of the Prodigal Son (Luke 15:11–31) the younger son had to go to the very depths before he would admit his sin and turn back. Proud humanity likes to build its own brave new world but it is a fantasy world doomed to constant failure. As the enemy gets closer there is a stubborn refusal to face facts.

Instead of conversion and turning to the Lord, arrogance led to an increasing disobedience to God's Word. Isaiah particularly spoke to the leaders of his nation who were misusing their solemn trust. Instead of guiding the people, they were leading them astray (verses 15 and 16). So we have this grim picture of God's wrath against a society which had become totally corrupt in its universal disobedience (verse 17).

Arrogance and disobedience will then inevitably lead to anarchy (verses 18–21). This is so much like the inspired commentary at the end of the Book of Judges which reminds us that 'everyone did as he saw fit' (Judges 21:25). Even brother would turn against brother (verse 21). But the final demonstration of man's failure is injustice. The end of chapter 9 shows the raw passions of jungle morality. The early verses of chapter 10 speak of the legalized wrongs of government. This is a familiar pattern in Scripture. For example, King Ahab was condemned by Elijah because he annexed the ground belonging to an insignificant individual called Naboth. But God cares for the rights of every person. In his sight that sin of Ahab was just as great as the idolatry and immorality also condemned. Jesus reminds us in moving words that we shall be judged as to whether or not we have shown our faith in love for our brothers (Matthew 25:31–46). The only way to avoid God's righteous anger is to turn back to his ways.

Questions

1. How far do we bring judgment upon ourselves and how far is it God's sovereign activity?
2. Look at the reasons for God's anger and apply them to modern society and even to the church.
3. Turn the negatives of chapter 10:1 and 2 into positives and see what it means for you.

The fall of Samaria

Samaria, also called Israel or Ephraim after its largest tribe, was the northern kingdom which separated from Judah after the reign of Solomon when the Kingdom of Israel was divided. It fell in 722 BC to the Assyrian army. Isaiah writes during the stormy period which marked the expansion of the Assyrian empire and the decline of the northern kingdom. Under Tiglath-Pileser III the Assyrians swept into Syria and Israel. In 733 BC the kings of Syria and Israel tried to pressurize Ahaz, king of Judah, into joining a coalition against Assyria. Instead, Ahaz decided to play politics and to ally with Assyria. This decision is condemned in Isaiah 7. Eventually, however, Assyria did assist Judah and conquered the northern kingdoms of Syria and Israel in 722 BC, making Judah even more vulnerable and preparing the way for the Assyrian invasion during the days of Hezekiah. See also the time chart on p.14.

Isaiah 10:5–34

God's control over history

Isaiah prophesies God's judgment and punishment of Assyria and again prophesies a remnant of Israel.

 God's control over history, including wars, is central to the Bible's message and is confirmed by our Lord himself (Mark 13:7). Later in Isaiah God speaks of 'Cyrus ... my shepherd ... [my] anointed', (44:28; 45:1). God can work through evil nations to accomplish his purpose. Isaiah realizes this truth as he ponders the onward march of Assyria up to the very doors of Jerusalem (verse 32). Likewise God was in control of Jesus' death at Calvary, using it to fulfil his purposes. 'By God's set purposes and foreknowledge', using wicked men (Acts 2:23), Jesus was crucified.

God is Lord of lords   (10:5–19)

God has a mission for Assyria beyond their expectation (verses 6–7). God, not the king of Assyria, will have the last word (verse 12). Judah is to be brought to its knees through God's use of Assyria (verses 10–11), by the dramatic events described in verses 28–32. Yet Assyria was still responsible for its acts of merciless aggression just as Judas, although a part of God's plan of salvation, was responsible for the betrayal of Jesus. The Assyrians' complacency (verses 8–11) will be judged as well as their pride (verses 12–14) and their sheer vandalism (verses 13–14). All who forget that they were made by and are subject to their Creator will fall (verse 15). The details of the punishment are outlined in verses 16–19 – a 'wasting disease'. (According to 37:36, 185,000 troops died in the siege of Jerusalem.) The long view of history proves that totalitarian despots inevitably fall.

God speaks through history   (10:20–34)

Judah is called 'a godless nation' in spite of all its religion (verse 6). When God has finished his work against Jerusalem (verse 12) and its punishment is complete, only a remnant will return (verses 20–23). This is Isaiah's constant theme. Here is the assurance of the final victory of the church with all its weakness and failure. God always preserves at least a remnant of his people against overwhelming odds. The chosen people will survive (see Malachi 3:16–18) and become part of the faithful nucleus awaiting and welcoming Jesus in spite of the solemn words of John 1:11–13. Paul quotes these verses from Isaiah in Romans 9:27 and 28 to explain God's dealings in salvation history.

Isaiah vividly describes the final downfall of Assyria, likening it to 'lofty trees ... felled' (verse 33) with no hope of renewal. In contrast, although the tree of Israel will be cut down, there will be 'A shoot ... from the stump of Jesse', a tree of Judah, which will spring to life again (11:1), a prediction of the coming of Jesus. God's purified people will have a new relationship with their Lord and 'truly rely on the LORD' (verse 20) with a genuine conversion experience (verse 21). This hope will bring courage in the days ahead (verses 24–25). The same God who delivered the Israelites in the days of Gideon and Moses will do it again (verse 26). At least in Isaiah's day Jerusalem will be safe, though even that city will one day fall. Outward situations will change and many aspects of the church will decay but the people of God are ultimately secure.

Questions

1. What does the teaching of this chapter say to Christians living in a country where they are being persecuted for their faith?

2. Has the concept of 'the remnant' anything to say in our present church context?

3. Relate verse 15 to your Christian service as an instrument in the hand of God. Do you sometimes fall into the category of verse 15 and forget your humble role?

Isaiah 11:1 – 12:6

God my salvation

Hope for the salvation of the world will spring from the remnant of Israel. This prospect prompts a song of praise (chapter 12).

 Before he launches into a series of messages to the nations Isaiah sums up his word of salvation hope. He promises that God is at work world-wide, words which have a new power for those who have met Jesus. The messianic kingdom offers hope even to the world of nature. Chapter 11:6–9 contains some beautiful imagery but it speaks also of nature transformed through the transformation of mankind.

A vision of the Saviour   (11:1–5)

This is an important passage in which Isaiah predicts the coming of the Messiah, 'a Branch', linking him with the house of King David, whose father was Jesse (verse 1). Both Matthew and Luke must have been aware of this prophecy, as both record genealogies tracing Jesus' ancestry back to David as evidence that Jesus was the Messiah and fulfilling one of the prophecies about his coming to earth. Luke and Matthew also record that the Spirit of God was on Jesus (Matthew 3:16; Luke 3:22, 4:1, 14) thus fulfilling Isaiah's prophecy that 'The Spirit of the LORD will rest on him' (11:2).

There will be a remnant in the house of David as well as in the nation. This must be a reference forward to Jesus. His ministry was always 'in the Spirit'. Fruitfulness is the work of the Spirit at all times. Jesus uses the analogy of the fruitful and non-fruitful vine; those belonging to him bear fruit (John 15:1–8). Paul lists the fruit of the Spirit in Galatians 5. The sixfold attributes of the Spirit were unique to the Messiah but Old Testament leaders such as Gideon or David (1 Samuel 16:13) knew the power of the Spirit to enable them to undertake specific tasks given to them. The Spirit's work is seen in a blend of power and wisdom. These gifts described in verse 2 are specially for leadership, that will in turn lead to righteousness and justice (verses 3b–5), so often lacking in Judah's leaders. Only the Messiah has supreme authority and complete consistency.

A picture of peace   (11:6–9)

We see here the hope of a new heaven and a new earth, referred to again in chapter 65:17 and 25 and expanded by Paul in Romans 8. These vivid metaphors speak of peace and safety as promised and yet so often denied in our society. There is no short cut to such a world. In Christ there can be variety without enmity, with the weak no longer a prey to the strong. The key to this idyllic picture is the 'knowledge of the LORD' (verse 9) which must precede true peace. All the promises of peace in verses 6–8 are 'in that day' (verse 10). Only when the Lord is fully known will peace fully come.

A story of power   (11:10–16)

Already we are anticipating the return of God's people from exile and Isaiah likens it to a second exodus (verses 11, 16). This liberating act will be a banner under which unity will overcome division and jealousy (verse 13) and lead to complete victory over their enemies (verse 14). Even if the immediate context is to the return from Babylon, there is the wider promise of the gathering of God's people in the final days (cf. Matthew 24:31). Always Isaiah reaches beyond his own people. All nations are envisaged in the blessing which will come with the Messiah (verses 10 and 12a). Some who have refused God will suffer (verse 14). But the glory of God's kingdom is that it transcends all national and other human barriers as John saw in his vision: 'a great multitude ... from every nation ...' gathered around the throne and the Lamb (Revelation 7:9).

A song of praise   (12:1–6)

Isaiah often turns to praise in the light of the truth he believes and proclaims. Worship and the Word are ever married. Isaiah rejoices at the ending of the estrangement between God and his people (verse 1), the end of fear (verse 2) and the end of want (verse 3).

Here is a source of true comfort (*cf.* 40:1) and renewed quiet confidence and trust. We praise God not so much for his gifts as for himself the Giver.

The song ends with praise of the glory of God. God's name will be revealed by his deeds. Not least he is known yet again as 'the Holy One of Israel' (verse 6). The world needs to know and see that God is king, and, as things are, that means that it will look to us, his church, for evidence of that rule. What does the world see?

Questions
1. How far do you take 11: 6–9 as literal and how far is it a picture of transformed society? Think through the implications for the Christian's concern for the environment.
2. If the Messiah rules by the Spirit how far are these marks of the Spirit seen in the life of the church?
3. Chapter 12 is a personal hymn of praise. Ponder the truths it proclaims. Can you make it truly yours?

7

MESSAGES FOR THE NATIONS
Isaiah 13:1 – 24:23

Isaiah 13:1 – 14:32

Satan in disguise

Prophecies against Babylon, Assyria and Philistia, all typical of godless nations.

Isaiah now turns to the nations surrounding Judah with specific prophecies for each (chapters 13–23). He begins with Babylon, which was to replace Assyria as the world superpower at the outset of the seventh century BC. Isaiah predicts Babylon's downfall in its turn (13:19). The king of Babylon has the look of Satan about him for he is always clever at disguises, even dressing up as an angel of light (14:12–15: see 2 Corinthians 11:14). Jesus may have been referring to these words of Isaiah when he spoke of Satan's fall in Luke 10:18. But the immediate meaning of the passage is the fall of Babylon, the city which was always a symbol of man's defiance against God from Genesis 11 to Revelation 18. All nations are under divine control whether they acknowledge it or not. The king of Babylon thought he was above God but he found himself 'brought down to the grave, to the depths of the pit.'

What Babylon is like

In Scripture, Babylon is always a symbol of unprincipled oppression which ultimately cannot succeed. There will be a final day of the Lord, a day of wrath (13:6–9). God wishes to bring to oppressed people relief from suffering and bondage (14:3), to give rest and rejoicing (14:7) and to bring joy to the world of nature (14:8). Judgment against the relentless aggressor is described in 14:5–6.

The theme of chapter 14:12–21 is the uninhibited ambition and pride of Babylon. The New Testament has a grim parallel in the story of Herod's downfall; because in his pride and arrogance he refused to acknowledge God (Acts 12:21–23). This is the sin of insolent pride (verse 13). The desire to be like God was the original sin implanted by Satan in the Garden of Eden (Genesis 3:4). It is the exact opposite of our Lord's humble self-giving (Philippians 2:5–8). The result of pride is to bring the proud down to the grave (verse 15 cf. the fates of Nebuchadnezzar and Belshazzer in Daniel 4:30–34; 5:18–30).

What will happen to Babylon?

The underworld is seen as eagerly awaiting its new inhabitants (14:9–11).

The leaders in the world (verse 9) are as weak as anyone else. Death is a great leveller (14:10 and 11) and the world marvels that high and low suffer the same fate.

But there is no fate in Scripture, only God's controlling hand. God is at work waging holy war (13:2–3; see Joel 3:9–10) and 'the Day of the Lord' now takes on a worldwide dimension (13:10–13) rather than referring specifically to the end of the Babylonian empire. Jesus quotes this passage when describing the signs that the end of the age is coming (Matthew 24:29). Babylon, once the jewel and glory of kingdoms (13:19), when overthrown will become the haunt of repulsive animals and be turned into swampland. God is at work in his world and man will not have the last word. Satan's followers always ultimately pay the penalty for their sin.

Questions

1. Trace the story of Babylon in Scripture and relate it to the fall of nations in history. (Look at Genesis 11:1–9.)
2. Death is both a leveller and divider in Scripture. How does your church bring comfort yet challenge when individuals face the reality of death in personal life or family?
3. Pride goes before a fall. Where does that truth hit you?

Isaiah 15:1 – 19:25

The Day of the Lord

More prophecies against godless nations: Moab, Damascus, Cush and Egypt.

 Amos used the phrase 'the day of the LORD' when speaking of the judgment day of God upon all nations, not least his own people (Amos 5:18, 20). Even nations which do not know God are known by him and are judged according to the light they have received (see Romans 2:1–16). But also these chapters give missionary hope to all ages. Moab (chapter 15) was east of the River Jordan and Dead Sea in present-day Jordan; Cush (chapter 18) is probably present-day Ethiopia or the Sudan. The great hope of Africa, Egypt (chapter 19), has often been a significant world power. Here the hope for all these nations is not to be a great power but to rest at the feet of the Lord.

God knows

Those who have sinned against God's people will not be forgotten. God is not mocked, so Moab (chapters 15 and 16) will be judged. In part, Moab is the story of opposition to the work and will of God coming from pride and conceit (16:6), while for Syria (Damascus) the theme is idolatry (17:8). In the New Testament Paul speaks out against the pride and foolishness of men and their idol-worship (Romans 1:21–25). He, too, reminds us that each person and nation will be judged according to the response to the truth they should have known. God is Lord of all nations and nothing is hidden from him.

God acts

The phrase 'in that day' is repeated frequently in these chapters. We feel a sense of pity at the fall of Moab and the heart cries out over their sufferings (15:5) while there is pathos in their empty worship (16:12). There is something tragic about that kind of empty response in the hour of need.

Likewise, Egypt will be brought to her knees before a new work of God can happen there (chapter 19). It is reminiscent of the story of the Exodus in the days of Moses. Pharaoh refused to acknowledge God and continued to harden his heart until the evidence of God's power in the deaths of the firstborn brought Pharaoh to his knees (Exodus 5–12). It was vital that the wisdom and the religion of Egypt should bow before the power and wisdom of God Almighty (cf. 19:12–15). Ultimately God will always bring down the pride of people and nations. History is littered with that truth, not least in the repeated fall of Babylon described in Scripture.

God heals

The final victory will be with the people of God. It is helpful to contrast the desolation of Damascus (17:9) with the remnant of Israel who survived and turned to the Holy One of Israel (17:6–7). But most of all God is seen as concerned with all nations, longing for them to turn to him. This is seen in the very dramatic language of chapter 19:16–25, especially verses 22 and 25.

There is a response of fear in 19:16 and 17 which leads in turn to submission (verse 18), to worship (verse 19), to fellowship (verse 23) and to acceptance within the family of God (verses 24–25). In this way the great promise to Abraham that 'all peoples on earth will be blessed through you' (Genesis 12:3) is being fulfilled and all the ends of the earth are seen as within the covenant of God. No more will the Jewish nation alone be the chosen people. This is the great Old Testament vision of the mission of the church which we must ever fulfil and which we see growing in the New Testament. All history will lead to the final day of the Lord when all nations will be gathered at the feet of Jesus.

Questions

1. Look at chapter 19:24–25. In the light of these verses how can you tackle any possible racism or national superiority within the church?

2. 'My heart cries out over Moab' (chapter 15:5). How far do you care in this way for lost people and races?

3. With the story of Egypt fear is the beginning of hope. What place does fear have in the Christian experience? What kind of fear is wrong?

Isaiah 20:1 – 22:25
Doors open and shut

More prophecies against godless nations, Egypt, Cush, Babylon, Edom and Arabia and, in a great climax, a prophecy against Jerusalem itself.

 These are chapters full of contrasts. God is in control of the rise and fall of nations. For Ashdod, a Philistine city on the Mediterranean (chapter 20) and Babylon (chapter 21) there is finality and no recovery. With Jerusalem (chapter 22) there is the alternating note of judgment and hope. The concept of doors which are open and shut (22:22) is taken up by John, who quotes this verse in relation to Jesus, with its words of assurance and challenge to the church in Philadelphia (Revelation 3:7–8).

The fate of nations
In chapter 21:9 and 10 appears again the scriptural theme of the fall of Babylon from which there will be no recovery. Then there is the very different picture of Jerusalem (chapter 22). Like his contemporary, Amos, in the opening chapters of his prophecy Isaiah brings the challenge of the rise and fall of other nations home to Jerusalem itself. One hundred years before the fall of Jerusalem a very vivid picture of it appears in this chapter.

A famine is predicted in 22:2b, the leaders of the nation go into exile (verse 3) and the whole structure of the city is in chaos (verse 10). Tragically all this would happen. The revelry of verse 2a contrasts with this final note of judgment. This contrast is taken up again in verses 12 and 13 with its ominous reminder that often in times of crisis there is a dedication to pleasure at all costs because of the insecurity of the future. There is nothing new in our world.

The fate of leaders

Not only is God in control of nations, he watches over their leaders and Christians need to pray for God's sovereign intervention in the leadership of the nations of the world. There is a contrast between Shebna who abuses his position of responsibility (verses 15–19) and his successor Eliakim (verses 20–25). A great historian commented that 'Power tends to corrupt and absolute power corrupts absolutely'. There are many illustrations of the corruption due to power in history and not least in biblical history. Shebna sadly was using his position to feather his own nest and his family's position. There would inevitably be the grim fall from grace (verses 17–19). It is possible to trace many similar situations in the Word of God, for example, Saul and Solomon in the Old Testament and Jesus' parable of the unmerciful servant (Matthew 18:22–35).

Eliakim, who replaces Shebna, in contrast is given lovely titles. He is called God's servant (verse 20) and he is seen as the father of his people (verse 21). This is the mark of genuine leadership, caring for others rather than for himself. But even he will fall from grace (verse 25). Even the greatest have no ultimate security. The picture of the key on his shoulder is a reminder of the responsibility that Christians have of opening or shutting the Kingdom to others. It is a picture used by our Lord himself (Matthew 16:19; 18:18) both to Peter individually and to the disciples in general. Wherever the gospel is preached there is a key opening the door and wherever the gospel is rejected there is a shutting of the door. Those who serve the Lord in the ministry of God's word have a solemn responsibility.

Questions

1. Consider the theme of the key and how it applies to Christian service and ministry.
2. In the light of these chapters what do you make of the state of our own nation and what is the answer to our grim position?
3. 'My servant ... your father'. These are phrases used of Eliakim. What do they say of your responsibility in any position of Christian leadership?

Isaiah 23:1 – 24:23

The end of the world?

A final prophecy against a godless nation, Tyre, is followed by a vivid picture of the Lord's devastation of the world.

 Christians are not the only ones to speak in terms of the end of the created world in these days, but it is often the theme of Scripture and is always seen as imminent. Here in chapter 23 the fall of Tyre, called 'the market place of the nations', is seen as a symbol of the end of a secure world. Tyre will have a brief respite but the end is near.

All hell let loose

The language in these two chapters reminds us of the closing chapters of the Book of the Revelation and Peter's words in 2 Peter 3 describing the day of the Lord. The created order will one day dissolve and the grim picture of chaos in verses 1–13 will become a reality throughout the world. There will be no immunity on that day and no national or personal insurance policies will be of any help then.

In 24:17–23 there is a picture of cosmic judgment which speaks of the whole world in turmoil. Our Lord used similar pictures of the sun being darkened and the stars falling (Matthew 24:10). These can be thought of in terms of political upheaval but equally they may refer to the literal end of the universe that we know. How foolish then to live as if this world were everything. The most grim scene of chaos and cosmic upheaval that our contemporary writers can depict will pale into insignificance before the reality of the end. But the end is not with hell but with the glory of heaven.

All heaven let loose

Isaiah is preparing to write prophecies full of vision and victory for the people of God and he gives a foretaste here in the midst of prophecies of destruction (24:14–16). There needs to be pain before birth (see 26:16–19). But there is resurrection hope even here in the Old Testament. We are beginning to see what the New Testament gives us in completion, the message of Easter hope.

So in chapter 24:13–16 there is the reminder of the remnant of God's people (see verse 13) who will be left and who will bring glory to God even in the day of cosmic chaos. It is not without significance that in the book of the Revelation the great Hallelujah chorus occurs when Babylon falls (Revelation 19). It is a reminder that the last word is with God and that man's pride will be brought low. For the people of God who suffer persecution and rejection this note of final triumph is of great significance. For a world which believes it can save itself, the challenge here is contemporary and desperately urgent.

Questions

1. What evidences do we see around us of the final end and, in the light of these, what should we do? (Look up Luke 21:28.)
2. How does the church begin to get the world to see the truth of the end of all things?
3. How do you respond when you hear Jesus say we should watch and pray (Matthew 26:41) in the light of impending judgment?

8

GOD'S FINAL VICTORY
Isaiah 25:1 – 27:13

Isaiah 25:1–12

The great liberation

Following the judgment and chaos of the last few chapters comes the order and light of the rule of God.

The lengthy message to the nations, with all its obscurities, is now ended. The main theme is obvious; God is in charge. Now all is seen in the setting of God's final victory. This is a victory chapter, a song full of praise to the Lord. Immediate problems are overcome (verse 10) but also the final victory over death itself is prefigured in verse 8. In the midst of opposing forces God is turning the world upside down.

Victory over tyranny   (verses 1–5)

The word 'ruthless' is repeated three times here. It sums up the world's tyrannies in every age. But God keeps to his plan (verse 1), and will not be frustrated (*cf*. 28:29). Until the final victory day there is the promise of protection (verse 4, *cf*. 32:2), not a promise of immunity from trouble but of ultimate safety, and this is promised for all. Then one day the ruthless enemy will fall (verse 2), bowing before God's people (verse 3) and with all his taunts silenced (verse 5).

Victory over death   (verses 6–8)

The last days are often described in the Bible as times of feasting, culminating in 'the wedding feast of the Lamb' (Revelation 19:9). This is referred to even in the Old Testament, here in verse 6 and in Psalm 23:5. Victory is often seen as the end of all that spoils on earth. Then comes the final celebration. It is a triumph of 'Jerusalem' over 'Babylon'; the phrase 'on this mountain' (repeated in verses 6, 7 and 10), stands for Jerusalem or the heavenly Zion.

Here indeed is the vision of chapter 2 being fulfilled at last. It is clear now that only in heaven itself will this promise finally be seen in full fruition. Note the repetition of the word 'all' in verses 7–8 and link it with the great prospect of the company of believers in heaven in Revelation 7:9.

In that final day the 'veil of mourning' (verse 7) will be gone because death itself, the last enemy, will have been defeated. The New Testament picks up this idea with clarity and triumph in 1 Corinthians 15:26 and Hebrews 2:14–15. This is to be no short-term cure but the death of deaths forever. Death which swallowed up will now itself be swallowed up. God's people and purpose will be vindicated and will last forever.

Victory over pride   (verses 9–12)

This song anticipates the final victory of those who wait in positive expectation (*cf.* 26:8 and 40:31). This is a song sung in hope but in the context of verses 10–12 where God's enemies will be defeated. Always in Scripture victory and judgment go hand in hand (for example, see 2 Thessalonians 1:5–10). The grim picture of seeking to swim through a sea of manure is one of great indignity for Moab. With it there is also a note of finality in verse 12. Part of the biblical picture of triumph involves the downfall of all God's enemies, those who in pride raise themselves against the Almighty.

Questions

1. Trace the theme of the conquest of death from this chapter and through the New Testament verses mentioned.
2. How does this chapter inspire your prayers for the world?
3. When you are called to praise God how far do you follow this kind of meaningful remembrance of God's activity? Or are you guilty of mindless praise?

Isaiah 26:1–21

The final victory

A song of praise, reflecting on human frailty and God's final triumph.

 We are singing again. There are similarities between this chapter and the words of Jesus in John 16:21–23: the reference to childbirth (verses 17–18), the 'little while' (verse 20) and the phrase 'in that day' (verse 1), all appear in the gospel passage. Out of pain comes joy. There will be destruction (verses 5–6) before the new city rises. The judgment of those opposed to God is described in verses 14 and 21. God has the last word and resurrection hope breaks through.

The endurance of God's city   (verses 1–6)

Jerusalem will be a strong city again but only strong in God. He is the Rock eternal (verse 4) and he is the one who humbles the proud and defeats the oppressor (verses 5–6). God takes the initiative in the final victory.

But man has to respond, opening the gates to make a home for the righteous and the trustworthy (verse 2). The only way to true peace then and now is to have absolute trust in God and to keep steady in that relationship. Peace, in the Hebrew understanding of the word, is not merely the absence of strife but the positive well-being of the personality and the people as a whole. In a world of strife here are the true peace people.

The patience of God's people   (verses 7–18)

Blessings often come only after patient waiting (verse 8) and judgment upon evil is often delayed (verses 11 and 14). God's ways include absolute justice and they promise a pathway which leads to a certain goal, not always an easy journey. This is the blessing which comes to those who have a deep desire for God, his name and his will. Strong commitment is called for (verses 12–13) since there is no short cut to blessings. God will lead his people to final victory (verse 15) but until then there will always be tension. There is a confession of failure and frustration but like the pain of child-birth it is the gateway to new life (verses 16–19).

Confidence in God's purposes   (26:19 – 27:1)

Here is one of the Old Testament's glimmerings of resurrection hope without which there can be no ultimate victory. Bodily resur-rection is anticipated here (verse 19, see Daniel 12:1–3). This pas-sage could be seen as a national revival as in the dry bones parable of Ezekiel 37. The dew speaks of dawn and this is the emphasis of these remarkable verses: new life.

In Scripture resurrection and judgment are linked together. Noah was a symbol of life through death and yet he experienced massive destruction. The narrative of our Lord's passion reflects the same black and white picture. Resurrection hope springs out of the awesomeness of his crucifixion. There will yet be years of suffering (verse 20) but God has the last word. Even the destruction of Judah is part of his activity in wrath. Then the blood of the martyrs will be avenged (verse 21 and 27:1) and all the powers of evil will finally bow the knee. As always in the writings of the prophets we stand poised waiting for the New Testament fulfilment in our Lord's vic-tory over Satan on the cross (Colossians 2:14–15) in the glory of his resurrection.

Questions

1. Once more trace the New Testament references given above, and see how God works out his purposes.
2. Look at the picture of a peaceful society in verses 1–6. How far is that a picture of your church?
3. There is a summary of personal commitment in verse 13. Can you make that your own today and what would it mean in practice?

Isaiah 27:1–13

Harvest home

The day of final judgment is seen as harvest day.

Leviathan (verse 1) is a mythical serpent-like monster which represents wicked nations such as Egypt. The picture of the serpent also speaks of the Devil's activity from the beginning of Scripture. Isaiah looks forward here to the last days when the process of destruction of evil has reached completion.

God's gardening (verses 1–6)

Isaiah returns here to the theme of God's vineyard (see chapter 5). Every day God cares for his vineyard which is a picture of Israel. Our Lord uses the same theme in John 15 as a picture of the church. The original plan is one of care and providential provision so that there might be good fruit. In order to achieve this there must be a pruning process since there can be no fruit without first the attention of the gardener's knife. The idea of pain in discipline in order to bring forth the good fruit of character is part of biblical teaching (see, for example, Hebrews 12).

Verse 6 has a messianic note (compare with 11:1, 10). From the root of Jesse will come the real fruit: Christ and the church. This is also a spiritual truth which is always relevant. If we wish to have good fruit then we must have the true root. There can be no life of holiness without a deep foundation in the Lord. Tragically all too often, in spite of God's care, he discovers the wrong kind of fruitage because the Devil has also been at work and we have been negligent.

God's gathering (verses 7–13)

There is a vivid contrast between what the Lord will do with his own people through chastening and what he does with the enemies of his people in final judgment (verses 7–13). There is a note of restoration from exile and the blessings of atonement (verse 13). Because there has been a dramatic destruction of idolatry, the new relationship with the Lord can be established. So these verses fill out the promise of verse 6 which has a universal scope. All the world will be blessed through the restoration of God's people. Isaiah is never far away from world mission.

Contrasted with that ultimate hope there is the desolate picture painted in verses 10 and 11. This could be a picture of Jerusalem before the revival of hope. Or perhaps, more helpfully, it is a picture of the enemies of God's people who remain abandoned and forsaken because they have not responded to their Maker and Creator. The barren language of these verses is in direct contrast with the fertility of the well-tended vineyard described in verses 2 and 3.

In verses 12 and 13 we see the promise of a final bringing together of the people of God from every part of the world. It may have an immediate reference to the return of the Jews from exile: it also links very clearly with the language of the New Testament which speaks of the Lord bringing together his own people at the final day when all the church will be gathered as one in the glory of the eternal kingdom (cf. Matthew 24:30–31).

Questions

1. Root and fruit go together (verse 6). What does this say about the importance of Christian morals being dependent upon Christian doctrine?

2. Much in Isaiah, as in this chapter, suggests a global judgment. How would you defend this idea to someone who claims that it is unfair?

3. This chapter reflects the importance of discipline in the Christian life. How do you react to the Lord's disciplining in your life?

9

POLITICAL CRISIS:
GOD'S HELP OR MAN'S?

Isaiah 28:1 – 31:9

Isaiah 28:1–29

Stop your taunting!

Introduced as a condemnation of the drunkards of Ephraim, this chapter goes on to pronounce judgment on those who mock the truth.

There is something sinister about taunting, whether on a football field or in our streets. Isaiah was at the receiving end and knew what it was to have fingers pointing at him. This chapter speaks of the cost of going God's ways instead of man's and stresses the simplicities of faith as opposed to the excesses of man. Traditionally it is believed that Isaiah was martyred by being 'sawn in two' by Manasseh, son of Hezekiah (cf. Hebrews 11:37). Here he suffers only the pain of ridicule as he dares to speak against the political intrigue of his national leaders. He does not retaliate in kind but he will pronounce judgment seen as God's 'strange work' (verse 21). Yet even under pressure he speaks mostly of hope (verses 5–6 and verse 16).

Mankind's folly exposed   (verses 1–6)

Isaiah reminds Judah of the humiliating fate of the northern kingdom. Samaria had been a beautiful city on a tree-lined hill but it is likened to a garland on a drunkard playboy's brow (verse 1). That glory would quickly fade before the Assyrian invasion at the behest of God. All this was in spite of the warnings of the prophets, not least Isaiah's contemporary, Amos, who spoke to the northern kingdom (Amos 4:1; 6:1). Using the picture of a crown, Isaiah contrasts the dying crown of the drunkards with the true glorious crown of Judah, the Lord Almighty. We are reminded again of the remnant, a theme central to this book, and once more heaven is in sight.

God's message mocked   (verses 7–13)

Now we have a vivid picture of leadership befuddled by wine.
Judah was going the way of her northern sister. Religious leaders
should be filled with the Spirit and not with wine (*cf.* Numbers
11:29 and Ephesians 5:18). Isaiah faithfully records the taunts of the
leaders as the mockers parody the words of the prophet about the
simplicity and morality of God's ways (verses 9–10). There is great
danger that arrogant, religious know-alls will reject God's consistent and simple truths. Isaiah throws their mockery back to them
(verses 11–13) and says that God will speak through the foreign
language of the invading Assyrian army so that his words really
will sound nonsensical. Words meant to save will become words of
doom. Verse 11 is quoted in 1 Corinthians 14:21 where speaking in
tongues is seen as relevant to an unbelieving congregation rather
than to believers. Believers need words in a known language to
convict, edify and strengthen. To reject the beauty of God's offer of
a resting place is fatal; a tragedy seen in the words 'but they would
not listen' (verse 12).

God's method explained   (verses 14–29)

God's 'strange' work (verse 21) will be seen in judgment. Scoffers
who are self-confident, trusting in political alliances or even in
deliberate flirtation with the occult, need to listen to God's words. If
his people will not listen to anyone else the Assyrian army will
'preach' to them in the strong language of verse 17. How pathetic it
is to put our trust in human activities! The short bed and the narrow blanket are ironic references to the inadequacy of all human
answers (verse 20). God hates fighting against his own people; he
prefers to defeat his enemies. Verse 21 refers to the Lord's crushing
victories over the Philistines, through David, at Baal Perazim
(2 Samuel 5:20) and the defeat of the Amorite alliance, through
Joshua at Gibeon (Joshua 10:10). As he defeated these armies so he
will defeat the Israelites. It can be seen as preparation for the ultimate work of salvation to be carried out by the Messiah.

God's saving work is described in verse 16 with its lovely Old
Testament picture of the Messiah as a foundation stone. This picture occurs frequently in the Bible (*cf.* Psalm 118:22; 1 Corinthians
3:11 and 1 Peter 2:4–7). The sure foundation is our only hope in the

day of testing, as our Lord indicates in his parable of the wise and foolish builders (Matthew 7:24–28).

God's sovereign work is illustrated in the agricultural parable of verses 23–29. God does not keep changing his mind but always works to a purpose. He speaks through events, and through these events he is carrying out his chastening purpose (verses 27–28): God always knows what he is doing (verse 29).

Questions

1. Consider the sin of drunkenness and the biblical passages which speak of it. What does it say about the church's attitude toward alcohol?

2. Drinking habits might be seen as a private matter, but is it a public concern if the nation's leaders are not always sober or not always moral in their behaviour?

3. How do you interpret the events of your own life which seem painful? Can you see them as part of God's providential work?

Isaiah 29:1–24

An act of mercy

Another prophecy of destruction followed by new life with prosperity given back to God's people.

 God's love for Jerusalem is revealed in these verses through Isaiah's own affection. The word 'Ariel' in verses 1 and 2 literally speaks of hearth and home. The promise of a last-minute reprieve may have reference to the immediate deliverance in 701 BC from the forces of Assyria. We are also given the lasting picture in poetic language of the eventual deliverance of God's people who will at last acknowledge the sovereignty of God.

Life from the dead   (verses 1–8)

There is a play on words in verses 1 and 2. Ariel, the hearth and home, becomes the picture of a burning furnace at the end of verse 2 with a hint of holocaust about it. There follow some solemn words about a people who go on rejecting God's mercy. It is a picture of David's city, Jerusalem, as it was meant to be and how, sadly, it had become. Again we may be reminded of our Lord's words as he wept over Jerusalem because it was rejecting his message and himself.

Yet we hear a voice as if from the dead (verse 4) and, in verses 5–8, we find that Isaiah has in mind more than a once-for-all event. Ultimately nobody can fight against the people of God and win. We may take this picture of the earthly Jerusalem in the Old Testament and link it with the Church of Jesus in our era.

Light from the darkness (verses 9–24)

The state of blindness described in verses 9–12 is a grim reality. Here is a people who are perishing without vision (*cf.* Proverbs 29:18). The prophets were meant to see clearly, but often they themselves had sealed eyes. The Old Testament is full of the condemnation of priests and prophets who had lost the vision of God. If leadership is without spiritual insight there is little hope for the people of God.

Religion without reality is often the theme of prophetic preaching (verses 13–14). Our Lord himself used these words speaking of the leadership of his day (Matthew 15:8–9). The blind were leading the blind with a blend of furtiveness and bravado (verses 15–16). Using the picture of the potter and the clay Isaiah describes how people believe they can act without God knowing and yet dare to argue against their Creator (*cf.* 45:9 and 64:8).

Then comes the great reversal where darkness is turned to light and barrenness to fertility (verse 17). Isaiah is looking forward to the creation of a people who will praise God, not primarily with lip but with life. Ultimately spirituality is a life of holiness in which we are to *live* to God's praise as well as to worship to his praise. Paul's message to the Ephesians (and us) is that we are to do everything 'for the praise of his glory' (Ephesians 1:12,14).

Questions

1. Ponder the truth that ultimately God's people are kept safe, and relate it prayerfully to the attacks of the world on the church worldwide today.
2. Our Lord used the words of verse 13 against hypocrisy in his day (Matthew 15:8). Where can you sense hypocrisy in the life of the church and your church?
3. The note of praise at the end of this chapter has within it a sense of awe and holiness. How far does your praise have these elements in the centre?

Isaiah 30:1 – 31:9

God also is wise

These two chapters carry warnings against relying on political and military alliances, but we learn a great deal about what God is like and what God does.

Our title is a great statement from chapter 31:2. Too many of Isaiah's contemporaries preferred worldly alliance to reliance upon God. Ironically they were going back to their old slave masters, Egypt, who would be useless (30:6b–7). It was part of a national lack of perspective. The rebellious attitude described in 30:9–11 is shown to be based on flimsy foundations (verses 12–14). Assyria will fall in God's time and way and this event will merge into the picture of the eventual collapse of all the enemies of God. In the hour of testing it is very important to know your God. He is a personal God (30:19–21) yet also a God of world-shaking judgment (verses 23–26).

What is God like?   (30:1–31:14)

Four truths about God are revealed in these verses.

1. God is holy

One of Isaiah's favourite titles for God is 'The Holy One of Israel', which is repeated in verses 11, 12 and 15. He also describes him as 'a God of justice' (verse 18b). Therefore to return to him will always involve practical repentance, a turning to his ways (30:22; 31:7).

2. God is powerful

He is depicted as a lion (31:4), which is used as a symbol of the Messiah (Revelation 5:15) and at the same time is likened to a lamb (Revelation 5:6; John 1:35), another important symbol for the

Messiah. God will never let go and nobody can ultimately make him change his purposes.

3. God is loving
He is full of compassion for those who are prepared to wait for him (30:18). In complete contrast to the image of the powerful lion, God is now depicted in 31:5 in the very tender picture of a mother bird hovering; compare our Lord's words about Jerusalem (Matthew 23:37).

4. God is wise
It is foolish not to consult God in the hour of decision. There are many stories in the Old Testament which illustrate this, not least Abraham waiting for a child, deciding to go his own way and producing from a slave girl the child Ishmael who could never be a substitute for Isaac. God has his plan and he will deliver Jerusalem in his time. We too need always to ask for wisdom from on high if we are to serve God fully (cf. James 1:5).

What will God do?   (30:15 – 31:9)
God's character is seen in action.

1. He will offer peace
Isaiah repeats (in verse 15) the offer of peace made earlier in chapter 26:3. True peace comes after repentance and is the opposite of the frantic busyness of the unbeliever (verse 16).

2. He will offer purpose
The promises of verses 19–21 are always true. Opposition will come but all in God's plan and purpose. We may make wrong decisions but he will call us back, often through teachers who are true to his Word and through God's Word by his Spirit in our lives.

3. He will offer prosperity
We must avoid the prosperity cult which is so often popular and misquotes Scripture. There is promise of a renewed creation in verses 23–26 (cf. 60:19–22). It is a promise of heaven; how else can you explain verse 26? But there are promises in Scripture for the

here-and-now, as in our Lord's promise in John 10 to give life abundant.

4. He will offer protection

Protection is the theme of chapter 31:5. It includes the note of a new passover with its similarity to that in the Exodus (Exodus 12). Men make decisions which often lead to disillusionment and disaster. To wait for God is the only true recipe for true safety and security.

Questions

1. Think of the character of God as a lion and a mother bird. How do we understand these two seemingly contradictory attitudes of our Creator and how do we reflect them?

2. Guidance is as important to a group of people as to the individual. How can we translate the promise of chapter 30:19–21 into the way we plan the future of our church?

3. The call in chapter 30:18 is to wait for him. What does that mean in the planning of your life, your time and your priorities?

4. Can the world ever find quietness and trust without repentance? How does this question reflect on religions other than Christianity?

10

SALVATION AND ITS DARK PRELUDE
Isaiah 32:1 – 35:10

Isaiah 32:1–20

The kingdom of righteousness

This is the fourth promise about a coming king, one who will lead his people to a restored humanity.

 In verse 10 calamity is foretold for the following year but the disaster described in verse 14 is bigger still. However, after disaster comes the promise of the pouring out of the Holy Spirit and promises concerning true peace in society (verses 15–20). Isaiah's vision here is more mature than the young man's hope of chapter 2.

A people at peace   (verses 1–8)

Much depends on the quality of leadership. In a leader there should be no conflict between public duty and private morality. This statement of righteousness and justice is repeated in verses 16–17. There could be no short cut to genuine peace (compare James 3:17–18).

The call here is for good people to be like a shelter and a rock, reflecting the character of God himself, as described in 25:4. The challenge is to stop the drift of sand and to become an oasis of life; to become like a refreshing stream in the desert. Once more the picture is linked with God himself (see 35:6–7; 41:18) and Jesus made the same point in John 7:37–39. It is challenging to recognize that what God is to us we are meant to be to others.

With good leadership will go good citizenship. Citizens will use their God-given faculties (verse 3) and discover new ones (verse 4). Then society will be in tune with God's moral order and not in conflict with it. We need to move away from concern for titles and status. Jesus taught that most clearly in his words about leadership within the church (Luke 22:25–30). We do well to pray for an end to our society being led by fools (verses 6 and 7).

The Prince of Peace   (verses 9–20)

God's rule will demand an end to complacency. The pampered ladies full of complacency will find their secure world disintegrating around them (verses 9–12). In worldly terms there is no guarantee of security: security comes only through God (verse 18). Plácing one's security in worldly things brings the danger of false hopes. Then as now people were escapist, trying to run away from reality: we need to repent of our part in this trend too. You can never impose peace on a corrupt society. A genuine revolution has to come first. No patching up will do because 'in that day' nothing will be secure (verse 14).

Now comes one of the Old Testament anticipations of Pentecost (verse 15: cf. Joel 2:28–32). With it comes the promise of abundance (cf. 44:3): 'The fruit of righteousness will be peace' (verse 17). That is a great statement for every age and is seen not least as fulfilment of the work of the Holy Spirit. In that context we have a wonderful picture of a biblical new age. This is a vision to encourage us to pray and work for biblical peace in society (see Zechariah 8:4–5). Such a vision calls for activism more than pacifism. Always it begins with repentance, clearing the ground, and then trusting God to do his own sovereign work.

Questions

1. Consider the unfolding of the promise of Messiah in chapters 7:14; 9:6; 11:1 and 32:1. How do these promises fit together and what do they tell us about the King?
2. The Bible never preaches peace at any price (but see Colossians 3:15). Peace and truth go together in these verses. How do we apply that principle in relationships within our church life?
3. Each person is called to be a 'shelter' and a 'refuge' (verse 2). In what ways can you become like this in your community?

Isaiah 33:1 – 34:17

The Lord is judge

When his people are most in need the Lord will rescue them, but those who defy him will be destroyed.

The attributes of God – judge, lawgiver, king and saviour (33:22) – are as applicable today as they were in Isaiah's day. The first part of this section is psalm-like in its style, expressing a longing for God in the midst of the trials the people are suffering. It was probably written at the time Sennacherib, King of Assyria, was threatening Judah (701 BC, see 36:1) and Isaiah foretells his defeat (33:19). Before his defeat, however, Judah has to suffer (33:7–9), but even its suffering pales into insignificance compared with the universal destruction described in chapter 34. It is seen as God's day of vengeance (34:8) and although the prophecy is specifically for Edom it can be seen to have universal application. For example, the picture of never-ending smoke (34:10), referring to Edom, is taken up by John to illustrate Babylon's downfall and total destruction (see Revelation 18:21 – 19:3, especially 19:3). The picture of burning sulphur (verse 9) is reminiscent of the destruction of Sodom and Gomorrah (Genesis 19:24) and the final day of judgment.

Present tension (33:1–9)

The grim reality of Isaiah's day is seen in verses 7–9 as a time of no hope; even brave men are reduced to weeping in the streets. Today we see similar scenes on our televisions from many parts of the world: people with no hope in the present, let alone the future. Travel and trade are destroyed and the land is desolate (verses 8–9, *cf.* Judges 5:6). But Isaiah does not run away from the truth, rather he is driven to fervent prayer (verse 2). It is a prayer based on belief in God's grace (*cf.* 30:18) and also his power over the nations (verses 3–4). Prayer can let loose very powerful forces. Read Revelation 8:1–5.

Like the Psalmist, Isaiah can quickly turn from prayer to praise because of who God is and what he does (verses 5–6). This is a theme which appears often in the Bible. God is a sure foundation and a source of wisdom and knowledge. Praise should never be mindless but focused on these eternal truths about God. This is a great strength in dark days.

Probing truth (33:10–16)
God is often represented in Scripture by fire: from the days of Moses and the burning bush (Exodus 3:1–6) and on Mount Sinai (Exodus 19:18); Elijah on Mount Carmel (1 Kings 18:37–38), Malachi (4:1) and on to the Day of Pentecost (Acts 2:3–4). Fire destroys (verses 11–14) and purifies (verses 14–16). God in his holiness cannot live with sin. He remains a 'consuming fire' destroying sin and purifying lives (*cf.* Deuteronomy 4:24 which the writer to the Hebrews quotes in Hebrews 12:29). Only those who are purified will survive (verse 15), the answer to the question at the end of verse 14.

Holy living is more important than ritual. This is the message of Micah 6:8 and Hosea 6:6 and the constant theme of Amos, all giants contemporary with Isaiah. Our thought-life matters supremely, hence the call to stop the ears and to shut the eyes against evil (verse 15). Only such a person would dwell with God and know security and fulfilment (verse 16). The pure in heart will see God (Matthew 5:8).

Permanent triumph (33:17–24)
Wonderfully, Isaiah gives us an assured glimpse of heaven itself and its king. His attributes are listed in verse 22 – judge, lawgiver, king and saviour (verse 17). Heaven is dominated by the judge who will end all who oppose God's purposes (verses 18–19). The picture is taken up in chapter 34 with its message of the day of God's wrath (verse 2) and the day of God's vengeance (verse 8), resulting in complete chaos (verse 10), foretelling the message in Revelation (for example, 34:4 is quoted in Revelation 6:14). But the Lord is also king, seen in his beauty in charge of a world of untroubled peace

(verse 17). In the midst of the new city (verse 20) we note the reign of the king (verses 21–22). Similarly the Book of the Revelation shows through the open door the lamb upon the throne (Revelation 4, 5). The ultimate definition of heaven, the dwelling-place of God, is to be 'for ever with the Lord'.

The city of verse 20 is the new Jerusalem, a city never to be seen in earthly history. Here is peace and security. Zechariah's vision of a city without walls was a symbol of it (Zechariah 2:3–4). What is now partial will become perfect and absolute in the new Jerusalem (34:20, 23–4).

Questions

1. What do these chapters tell us about heaven? How far should we seek to see these ideals on earth and how much will always be 'not yet'?

2. Is it right to see warfare and genocide today as pointing to the nearness of the coming judgment? Why?

3. Look at the quality of life described in 33:15 and judge your own daily life by it.

Isaiah 35:1–10

The joy of the redeemed

A prophecy of the blossoming of the desert and the return of God's people to the Promised Land.

 This chapter is sandwiched between the descriptions of the desert waste of chapters 33–34 and the war-sickness of chapters 36–39. Here is a true oasis (see verse 7a). It is gloriously poetic and prepares for the theme of the second part of the book with its emphasis on return from exile.

It is true prophecy in all its dimensions and looks on to the final day (verse 4) and everlasting joy for the redeemed (verse 10). The hinge of the chapter is the coming of the King himself (verse 4) and the coming of the Kingdom.

The coming of the King   (verses 1–6a)

A parched desert bursts into flower after rainfall and for a brief period is carpeted with flowers (verse 1). Isaiah describes how it will be for the redeemed in Zion (verse 10). Nature is used as a picture of God's activity for his people. Often Isaiah personifies nature, for example, Bashan and Carmel are likened to trees dropping their leaves (33:9), while mountains, forests and trees 'burst into song' for joy at what the Lord has done (44:23 and 55:12). Nature is not to be worshipped but should be seen as an enrichment of the glory of the Lord.

The writer to the Hebrews quotes verse 3a as an encouragement to Christian hope in the day of testing (Hebrews 12:12). Christians also need determination and a call to 'Be strong' (verse 3b). In the difficult days after taking over from Moses, Joshua was given the same command frequently by God (Joshua 1:6, 7, 9 and 18). It is easier to become strong when we are aware of God's activity. There is a promise for the future in verse 4b (*cf.* chapter 61:2) and a reference to the day of vengeance. In Scripture there is often a double note when looking forward to divine intervention, both judgment and salvation.

God brings enrichment, encouragement and enlightenment. Verses 5–6 herald the Messianic age. The events foretold here were fulfilled in Jesus' ministry (see Matthew 12:22) and in the days of the early church (Acts 3:7–8). The primary reference is to spiritual renewal (*cf.* 42:7). Jesus himself when healing a man blind from birth (John 9) also used the opportunity to highlight the tragedy of those who are spiritually blind.

The coming of the kingdom   (verses 6b–10)

There is a picture of the way of holiness in verse 10. It is in part a prophecy foretelling the way back from the Israelites' exile in Babylon, but it is also a symbol for the way back to true Christian living. Linked with it is a note of fruitfulness and greenness which reminds us of the picture of the fruit of the Holy Spirit both in Paul's writings (Galatians 5:22) and in Jesus' words on the importance of the vine bearing fruit (John 15:5–8).

There is an echo of the wilderness wandering in verse 6b. The water from the rock reminds us of Exodus 17:6. God can transform every wilderness experience. With the promise of fertility goes the promise of security. The 'Way of Holiness' is safe (verses 8–9), and is set apart for the holy and the redeemed. It is like the narrow way in the teaching of Jesus (Matthew 7:14) with its emphasis on choice (Jeremiah 21:8). It is only safe for the people of God. The wild beasts are banished (unless the faithful stray off the right path). Once more the Exodus theme appears; this is the way of those who have been liberated from bondage (verse 10).

The 'Way of Holiness' is echoed in Jesus' statement 'I am the way' (John 14:6) and the early Christians were known as followers of the Way (Acts 9:2; 19:9, 23).

The Way leads to Zion and to celebration (verse 10, which is repeated word for word in 51:11). There is laughter and joy for those who sow in tears (see Psalm 126) and that principle does not change. In verse 10 gladness and joy are personified (*cf.* Psalm 23:6). We are promised that there will be no more tears and sorrow, a future hope with its anticipation of the glory of heaven where alone all this can find fulfilment (*cf.* Revelation 21:4).

Questions

1. In these verses, which of these promises are for the future awaiting the glory of heaven, and which can we expect 'now'?
2. A church contains both weak and strong Christians. In your church how can the strong help the weak to be strengthened (verses 3–4)?
3. There is a recurring theme of joy in this chapter. How far are you reflecting that joy in your daily life?

11

GOD TESTS
HIS SERVANTS
Isaiah 36:1 – 39:8

Isaiah 36:1 – 37:38
The eleventh hour

Sennacherib, king of Assyria, threatens Jerusalem. King Hezekiah calls for Isaiah who prophesies that Jerusalem will be spared. Hezekiah prays and Sennoacherib is defeated.

 We come to the historical climax of the first part of Isaiah's book. There are two great tests for a good king: invasion of his realm and personal illness. Here, also, is a summary of the biblical teaching of a remnant looking forward. It is in the context of a vivid three-way conversation between the commander of the Assyrian army, the king and the prophet. The people of Jerusalem are significant silent spectators of the drama.

The voice of propaganda   (chapter 36)

Chapter 36 gives us an illustration of the technique of the act of subversion. The place of the meeting is ironic. It takes place at the same spot where Ahaz failed to believe God's promise (chapter 7:3). The Assyrian leader makes very skilful use of half-truths. He is right about the uselessness of Egypt (verse 6 *cf.* 30:1–2). He is right about the failure of other gods (verses 19–20). But he is wrong to put Jehovah in the same category. There is a clever blend of ridicule (verse 8), threats (verse 12) and cajoling (verses 16–17). There is subtlety in the misrepresentation of Hezekiah's reforms (verse 7). Even Isaiah's preaching is known and misconstrued (verse 10: *cf.* 16:6–13). The king's advisers are pathetic in their reply: all they are worried about is that the people will hear what is said (verse 11). The silence of the people (verse 21) is much more effective when it goes with repentance (verse 22; 37:1).

The voice of prayer (37:1–20)

Here is a model of the right response to a threatening situation, not with blind optimism but in the context of repentance. Later Hezekiah will pray himself but at first he understands the real value in leaning upon his prophet Isaiah for support. The king shows himself to be a man of vision (verse 3) in likening their situation to the birth-pangs of suffering. He is longing for a new order and feels they are almost there. Faith is limited but very real. God is invited to note the insults of the enemy. Hezekiah's prayer for the remnant (verse 4b) suggests that he has been listening to his prophet preacher. How vital to have a man like Isaiah to be able to pray for you (cf. Psalm 99:6).

From Isaiah comes a call to trust God's Word again (verse 6). The promise of ultimate triumph in verse 7 would strengthen the king to face a new war of nerves (verses 9–13). Then the king himself resorts to prayer, neither ignoring the threats nor giving in to them. (The same spirit is seen among the persecuted apostles at their prayer meeting (Acts 4:29).) Hezekiah appeals to the creator God (verse 16) acknowledging his authority over all and asks God to note everything Sennacherib has said (verse 17 cf. 1 Kings 8:52). Even as he prays, the situation clarifies as Hezekiah recollects that other gods are no gods: God alone is God. Crises can clear the mind remarkably.

The voice of promise (37:21–38)

There follows a vivid triumph song from the Lord to Sennacherib with a taunt typical of such songs in verse 22 and the solemn words from the Holy One of Israel in verse 23. Assyria is reminded that she is only a tool in the hand of God (verse 26). Her pride will be judged (verses 24–25), and God will have the last word (verses 28–29). The end of the chapter tells us that God's intervention was in the form of a plague that devastated the army of Assyria. This event is also recorded in historical records, as well as in the Bible.

Judgment will come to Judah but a remnant will survive. Soon life will return to normal (verses 30–32), and Jerusalem, for the moment, will be safe (verses 33–35). There is no absolute security for any earthly place and later on Jeremiah will proclaim the ultimate downfall of Jerusalem. Happily the new Jerusalem is an inheritance utterly secure (*cf.* 1 Peter 1:4). Twenty years later the events prophesied in verse 38 happened and the king of Assyria was murdered at prayer. His end was similar to that of Belshazzar (Daniel 5) and Herod (Acts 12). You do not defy God and survive. The contrast between Sennacherib's prayer leading to judgment and Hezekiah's penitent prayer leading to blessing (verse 1) is very marked and challenging.

Questions

1. This story shows God's intervention at the last moment. Think of other illustrations in history when this has been true and give thanks.
2. Read Hezekiah's prayer. What can you learn from it about intercession?
3. Hezekiah's response to the Assyrians is a vivid illustration of how to meet verbal abuse. How do you cope when you have been misrepresented?

Isaiah 38:1 – 39:8

A miracle and its aftermath

Hezekiah is ill but prays and is healed. He receives envoys from Babylon and shows them all his treasures, unconcerned that he is storing up disaster for his descendants.

We move on to the second dramatic test of Hezekiah's faith. It provides a remarkable illustration of the power of prayer and the place of the prophetic word. The result, however, was not an unmixed blessing. This is seen in the dubious activity of the king in chapter 39 and his attitude towards 'peace in my time' (39:8; implying that he was unconcerned whether warfare should come after his death). This story is the account of a biblical experience. The truth of Scripture and the experience of God's activity in our lives ought to correspond for us and form a continuous whole.

Experience of God's renewal   (chapter 38)

Isaiah records here the dramatic events of Hezekiah's illness (verses 1–8) and recovery (21–22). It has been suggested that the plague which killed the Assyrian army also affected Hezekiah, the boils being a symptom of plague. Hezekiah and God have a dialogue with the help of Isaiah's personal intervention. God's intention is clearly stated: Hezekiah will die (verse 1). The prophet is absolutely honest and he calls the king to put his house in order. Similarly the 1662 Book of Common Prayer calls upon the Church of England vicar, in visiting the sick, to remind them of their need to make a will. It seems a macabre thing for a visiting minister to do but it reminds us of the responsibility we have for our lives and our property. Hezekiah had a particular concern for the succession to the throne since as yet he had no heir. Manasseh was not yet born, as

99

can be seen from 2 Kings 21:1. Hezekiah's claim of loyalty (verse 3) was very genuine (2 Kings 18:3–6; cf. 1 Kings 11:4) and he had rooted out idolatry (cf. 36:7). He is not claiming favour based on good works, but he has an expectation that God does reward those who serve him. His sheer humanity is displayed by his bitter weeping.

Prayer changes things, and a new word comes from the Lord (verse 4). It is a challenging reminder of how important prayer is. The new promise from the Lord (verses 5–6) gives Hezekiah fifteen more years of life, and the sign of the sun's shadow going back was given by God himself (verses 7–8, cf. Joshua 10:12–14). Yet alongside the divine intervention there was the human remedy of the poultice of figs (verse 21). Miracles and medicine need not contradict each other.

Then Hezekiah reflects poetically on the incident with Job-like candour (verses 9–20). Hezekiah's personal experience becomes part of corporate worship ('we will sing', verse 20). His complaint (verses 10–14) is honest but hopeless because he has no knowledge or hope of resurrection. Death is seen to have the last word (verses 10 and 18). Yet Hezekiah knew that God was in control, even of suffering (verses 13–15). This remembrance of God's activity leads to a section full of praise for God's deliverance (verses 15–20). Even in praise there is a reminder that suffering is part of the divine plan (verses 16–17). Without knowledge of life after death, this man is learning through experience. Not least he has discovered the assurance of sins forgiven and forgotten (verse 17b). The same assurance is given in Micah 7:19, Psalm 103:12 and Jeremiah 31:34 which tell us that God puts our sins out of sight, out of reach, out of mind and out of existence.

An experience of God's rebuke (chapter 39)
From the heights of Hezekiah's song of praise and knowledge of sins forgiven there is now the record of his fall from grace. The visit of the king of Babylon's envoys is a reminder that the second part of the book of Isaiah is concerned with a new enemy on the horizon. Hezekiah's faith, which had been proof against illness and the threat of siege, gave in to flattery, seen in the king's reply to the prophet (verses 3–5). The king of Babylon was using the envoys' visit to hide his subtle investigation of Hezekiah's situation. Likewise the Devil loves to work in such devious ways.

This picture of the world at work is matched by God's word at work. Once more Isaiah is honest in his message to the king. The man of faith can see further ahead than the man of affairs. There will be a price to pay for Hezekiah's folly which is the backcloth to the next chapters, bringing with them the warning of exile. The final chapters will reveal the wickedness of Hezekiah's son but it is clearly forecast in verse 7. Hezekiah's response accepts God's verdict but with little concern for the future (verse 8). Isaiah, the prophet, would live with a burden on his heart till he could write the rest of the book. He would speak to the heart of God's people (40:2) with a promise of hope beyond judgment and exile. Hezekiah was only concerned for peace in his life-time. The prophet was concerned for a peace for all time which would come only after suffering. He would proclaim a Prince of Peace who was also the Suffering Servant.

Questions

1. Consider God's apparent change of plan when Hezekiah prays (chapter 38:2–6). What does it say about the power of prayer? How do you relate it to God's changelessness as proclaimed in Numbers 23:19?
2. Suffering is seen as part of God's programme in chapter 38:17. In your church do you see this as being as much a part of God's work as the ministry of healing?
3. Hezekiah seems happy with peace in his time. How much do you care about the effects of your actions on a generation to come?

Miracles

Miracles do not occur consistently in Scripture. They centre around special moments of God's activity as with the narrative of Moses and Joshua, or Elijah and Elisha and supremely in the ministry of Jesus, spilling over into the Acts of the Apostles. The Bible does not differentiate between God's general activity in providence and his special intervention in the miraculous.

Sometimes it is possible to explain miracles in a scientific manner. In such cases it is very often a matter of divine timing, as with the parting of the Red Sea (Exodus 14) or the River Jordan (Joshua 3), or the presence of the manna in the wilderness (Exodus 16). Some have sought to explain the particular miracle in Isaiah 38 by the refraction of light. Scripture's emphasis is that God has in his own sovereign way spoken through an event which is out of the ordinary.

In our Lord's ministry the miracles are seen as 'signs and wonders'. They speak of a truth and they demonstrate the person of Christ. He himself spoke sternly against those who merely wanted miracles and looked for a wonder-worker (cf. Matthew 12:38–39).

Jesus himself as God-man is a miracle in action. The resurrection is the supreme miracle without which our faith is vain. Spiritual rebirth is always the greatest miracle of all. It may be significant that on one occasion, when people brought a paralyzed man for healing, Jesus offered forgiveness in the first place and used the healing as a demonstration that he had power to forgive (Mark 2). A miracle will always point to a greater truth.

12

PREPARING THE WAY FOR THE LORD
Isaiah 40:1–31

Isaiah 40:1–11

Many voices, one song

A prophecy of comfort and strength for Jerusalem and a call to prepare the way for the Lord's coming.

In the second part of his prophecy (see *How many Isaiahs?* page 16) Isaiah takes a long view as he anticipates Judah's exile in Babylon and their eventual return. It would come as a contemporary word of hope to those in exile as still it comes to us. This is a very personal section (verse 1, 'my people ... your God ...'). God is calling his people back into a loving relationship with him. There is a musical atmosphere about these verses with many voices blending in song. It is a call to the people as well as praise to God.

A word to the heart   (verses 1–2)

A word of tender grace comes first from God (verse 3) anticipating his promise to lead his flock (verse 11). The first words are words of comfort reminding us of Jesus' description of the Holy Spirit as the Comforter or Counsellor (John 14:12; 15:26; 16:7 AV). To speak tenderly is the language of wooing love, speaking to the heart. True religion must always grip the heart. There must always be a personal element at the heart of faith. But our faith is also a matter of triumphant grace, more than mere feelings. It is based on the proclamation of God's favour (*cf.* Luke 2:14). The loving whisper of verse 2a becomes the loud cry of the next verse. A message must be proclaimed to the people of God which has three finished actions – completed, paid for, received (verse 2). The message is the promise of return from exile because Israel has paid the price of her sin, has been forgiven and now the slate has been wiped clean.

A word to the hands   (verses 3–5)

God promises action to demonstrate his grace and we must respond. The prophecy in verse 3 was claimed by John the Baptist in his unique ministry in preparing for the coming of Christ (Mark 1:2–3; John 1:23). But this task of preparing the way is for us all. God himself will turn everything upside down (verse 4) and we must commit ourselves to prayerful service in his cause. Mary was obedient to God's call to be the mother of the Messiah (Luke 1:38, 46–55) and, like her we must be ready for the call and revolution in our lives which will demand work as well as prayer. There are no mountains too high for God nor for the people of faith. The glory of the Lord promised in verse 5 will be seen in the deliverance of Israel from exile, as they were delivered from Egypt during the Exodus, and, looking forward to the New Testament, deliverance at Calvary through the resurrection and the second coming of Christ. There God's glory will be seen in the fullest measure and we may play our part in proclaiming that message in loyalty to the King.

A word to the soul   (verses 6–8)

All human achievement is overshadowed by the brevity of life and certainty of death and we are reminded in verses 6 and 7 of the impermanence of life (*cf.* Psalm 103:15–17). All great leaders must come to the end of their life on earth, even Moses, Elijah or David, and cannot be relied on forever. In exile Israel lacked that great leadership which had been available to them formerly and had to learn to lean more upon God himself. Sometimes crisis moments put our perspectives right. In contrast with the world's transience is the permanence of the Word of God; verse 8b is echoed by Jesus in Matthew 5:18 and Mark 13:31. Peter quotes verses 6–7 in 1 Peter 1:24–25, assuring Christians that they are born again by the Word of God whose power never fails. We need to make God's Word central in our lives if we are to return from a spiritual exile not only as individuals but as churches.

A word to the lips   (verses 9–11)

The good news of restoration needs public airing. Christians are very good at offering loud praises to God in church but are much less vocal when facing an unbelieving and questioning world. We should sing constantly of God's power and also speak of it. Only God could have empowered his exiled people to speak of good news. We know even more of that power as we rejoice at the resurrection miracle of God. But this power of God (verse 10) is linked beautifully with his tender love (verse 11). Here is a gentle picture of the shepherd leading his sheep with all the qualities of loving concern for the individual within the flock. It is the theme of Psalm 23 and John 10 and is a challenge for every 'under-shepherd' of the sheep. There is nothing soft about this picture, for the shepherd is a leader who risks his life for the sheep's protection and safety.

Questions

1. Is the world becoming more or less prepared for the second coming of Christ? How much do we have to do and how much do we leave to God himself?
2. In what way is your church mobilized to proclaim the good news to those yet outside? How do you rate this as a priority compared with the quality of your worship and praise?
3. If the Word of God is the abiding reality, what plans have you to make it more central in your life? What will that involve?

Isaiah 40:12–31

I believe in God

Isaiah tells the people that their idea of God is too small and he ridicules their idol worship. The real God has created us, reigns over us and cares for us.

 The dominant themes of this passage are the awesome greatness of God the creator and the complete inability of his people to understand who he really is: 'Do you not know? Have you not heard? ... Have you not understood since the earth was founded?' (verse 21). The evidence of his greatness is before their eyes (verse 26) and yet they don't understand him.

The God who creates   (verses 12–20)

This is a passage full of beautiful poetry in which God shows his people that he is the creator of all. He is so great that he can 'measure the waters in the hollow of his hand' and measure the heavens 'with the breadth of his hand' (verse 12). 'Because of his great power and mighty strength, not one [star] ... is missing' (verse 26). The majesty of the true God includes not only perfect knowledge (verses 13–14) but also infinite power (verse 22). No one can understand God's mind, no one has needed to teach him anything and to him 'all the nations are as nothing; ... worthless'. The history of mankind is in his hand (verse 17: *cf.* Paul's affirmation in Acts 17:24–26) and we should read history with the Bible in our other hand.

Contrasted with this picture of the true God and his majesty is the poverty of false gods. Isaiah loves to satirize, to destroy by ridicule. It is a dangerous weapon, but the prophet is not afraid to use it (*cf.* 44:9–20; 46:1–7). Verses 18–20 present a picture all the more ridiculous because it is flanked by two paragraphs full of the glory of the true God. Idolatry and its worship is never beautiful. When Paul visited Athens he was upset by what he saw as the Athenians' idolatry, not captivated by the artistry of their man-made idols. Idolatry is condemned consistently in Scripture from the days of the Ten Commandments onwards. Yet it remains always a scourge of God's people because of the influence of surrounding nations and their religions (Hosea 14:8; 1 John 5:21). Modern idols may be more sophisticated but they are equally dangerous and ludicrous.

The God who reigns   (verses 21–26)

The Creator God has not left his world. The great novelist Thomas Hardy thought that if God existed he was like a watchmaker who had wound the world up but was letting it run down. Isaiah knew better. He sees God as still on his throne, that is, in control (verse 22a), a memory still fresh from his vision in the temple (chapter 6). Such a theme can make sense of the apparent victory of evil in the world (*cf.* Habakkuk 2:20). There is great power in the description of a God who knows each star by name (verse 26). Such a God can be trusted to know our deepest needs. Jesus would pick up the theme of the God of all creation being the Father of his people (*cf.* Matthew 6:25–32). To understand this picture we need to lift up our eyes from earthly things and look upwards to God, the creator of the heavens (verse 26). All too often our perspective is too earthbound. God is supreme in nature and sovereign over history. In verses 22–24 he is seen to be the King of kings. Leaders and nations come and go but he remains. It is a constant theme of Scripture that rulers often need to be humbled with an awareness of God's sovereignty (see the book of Daniel). But the message comes as a great relief to all who suffer in exile or through the whim of totalitarian rulers.

The God who sustains   (verses 27–31)

God is not too great to care. Isaiah's poetry comes to a practical climax, as all profound theology should. God cares more for us than for stars. Mankind is the summit of his creation. In the account of the creation the fact that 'he also made the stars' is almost lost among the list of all the wonders created by God (Genesis 1–2). The Jews in exile will not be forgotten nor is their God fickle (verses 27–28).

If he is not too great to care he is, however, too great to fail. This is a gentle rebuke for not trusting God's strength. Our response should be to put our hope and trust in the Lord (verse 31: see 25:9 and 30:18). Then comes that promise which caps all promises (verses 29–31). This is no anticlimax. Our God is a God who cares for the practical. George Adam Smith has this incisive comment on this great verse; 'Let hope rejoice in a promise which does not go off into the air but which leaves us upon solid earth'.

Questions
1. History is under God's control. Think of the history of your nation and see what God may be saying to you in your contemporary world situation.
2. Consider modern forms of idolatry. How can they creep into our church life and worship?
3. Make verse 31 a personal meditation and prayer. Where are you being asked to soar with vision, to run with consistency, to walk with patience?

13

GOD STATES
HIS CASE
Isaiah 41:1 – 42:17

Isaiah 41:1–16

Let God speak

This chapter is set in the courtroom. God challenges the world concerning his sovereignty.

 The prophet claims that God is in charge of world-shattering events such as the appearance and victorious march of Cyrus (verse 2), who is seen as an instrument in God's hands (verse 4, see 44:28) as was Assyria (10:5). When events in the world are rightly interpreted God speaks.

God speaks to the nations   (verses 1–7)

The call here is to face facts and not indulge in escapism. Jesus taught us that there would always be wars and rumours of wars so that we should be prepared (Matthew 24:4–8). Here in verses 2 and 3 there is a picture of the relentless march of the army of Cyrus 200 years before the event took place: he is named in chapters 44:28 and 45:1. One day the fear of the Babylonians will end when the Babylonian empire will be toppled by Cyrus and the Jews will return from exile (Ezra 1).

But facing facts also helps in facing fears. The reaction in verses 5–7 is understandable and is universal. The prophet points out the pathos of trying to help your brother with nothing but empty words or building useless idols. We need ruthlessly to expose the emptiness of the world and its message when facing the storms of life.

The heart of this passage is in verse 4 where God enables Cyrus to free his people so that they can face the future. The very name of Jehovah (translated as the LORD) speaks of his unchanging character and trustworthiness. The picture of the first and the last is taken up again in Revelation 22:11–12. God has absolute control over the affairs of men and nations.

God speaks to the church   (verses 8–16)

This paragraph begins with a typical biblical phrase used when wanting to contrast something: 'But you'. We see also the introduction of an important theme in the book of Isaiah, God's servant (verse 8). It starts with the picture of Israel as God's servant and moves to the classic chapters which deal with the Suffering Servant, a concept which is fulfilled finally and supremely in Jesus. The immediate thrust of these verses is to remind us that Israel is God's chosen people and God is at work in testing and purifying his people for service through the events happening around them. We see in verses 8 and 9 a clear purpose in God's activity. This active sovereignty is not an abstract idea but rather a very personal and pastoral picture. Israel is seen here as God's servant, 'the descendants of Abraham my friend', but Jesus said to his disciples 'I no longer call you servants ... I have called you friends' (John 15:14–15). Ultimately God has chosen and therefore the outcome is certain (cf. John 15:16). There is nothing special about Israel, but Israel's God is very special.

This leads to the great promise of verse 10: 'I am with you'. This great promise can be traced through Scripture enabling the servants of God to launch into almost impossible tasks (as did Gideon [Judges 6–8] or the disciples [Matthew 28]). In verse 10 we find assured protection in the picture of God's right hand, as a hand of might; in verse 13 God takes hold of Israel's right hand in a gesture of love. Many a minister has used this verse to speak of the hands joined in marriage as a symbol of the relationship between the Lord and his people. The joining of three hands at the climax of a marriage service is a symbol of lives joined by God and secure in him. Ultimately, whatever the circumstances may be in our personal life or in the world around 'those who are with us are more than those who are with them', as Elisha's servant found when his eyes were opened (2 Kings 6:16).

Verses 14–16 describe the offer of God's power which will often be found in the midst of weakness. The picture of Israel as a worm (verse 14) is of her insignificance and unworthiness. But God will transform her (verse 15) and give her power and authority. The source of this authority is the God who calls them, the Redeemer and Holy One of Israel (verses 14b,16). True power in the Christian

113

life is always seen in the midst of weakness. Here is no easy comfort but the strong comfort of God's word for us to receive and then to convey to others in days when all other confidences seem to evaporate.

Questions

1. Consider the titles of God – Servant (in chapter 42), Redeemer, Holy One of Israel. How do they link together?
2. The theme of power in weakness is constant in Scripture (*cf.* 2 Corinthians 12:7–10). What does this say to us about the kind of power we should like to see demonstrated in our church?
3. The phrase 'do not fear' comes three times in verses 10, 13 and 14. It seems to link with the promise in verse 10: 'I am with you'. How do you personally link the promise with the command?

Isaiah 41:17–29

God in action

God silences the pride of the people not by argument but by showing them what he has done.

 This section begins with a great promise for the people of Israel – God will supply all their needs and will never forsake them (verses 17–20). The whole tenor then changes as God challenges the idols and idolators. Not one has been able to predict future events so therefore the people could not say 'He was right' (verse 26). Only God has been able to foretell future events. Isaiah likens the idols to 'wind and confusion' (verse 29).

God acts in concern for his people   (verses 17–20)

The promise of true riches for the people of God after the poverty of exile is described in very beautiful language. Thirst will be satisfied (verse 17), a reminder of Jesus' promises in John 7:37–39. Loneliness will be met by the presence of the Lord (verse 17b). Barrenness will turn to fruitfulness (verses 18–19). Here is God's overflowing provision which is seen in both spiritual and in material terms. Coming home to the Promised Land will mean more than material prosperity. In the New Testament this theme is taken up in Paul's concept of abundance, overflowing blessing, more and more. So he promises in Philippians 4:19 that God will meet all our needs 'according to his glorious riches in Christ Jesus'.

There is also an overriding purpose in God's provision (verse 20). Blessings are meant to spill over to others. What God does for his own people should lead the nations to consider and turn to the Lord. Psalm 126 which was written after the exile shows the fulfilment of these promises. At momentous events people ask what God is doing. So it was on the Day of Pentecost; so in the Old Testament the magicians of Egypt, unable to compete with Moses' miracles, acknowledged that this was the finger of God (Exodus 8:19). God is at work.

We are not called, however, to sit back and bask in what God has done. We are meant also to testify by life and lip to the goodness of God in our lives (cf. 1 Peter 2:9–10). Our lives should demonstrate clearly the reality of which the lip should speak boldly. This is the beginning of evangelism, the experience of the church leading others to seek and find. So Jesus in the upper room speaks of what the Spirit will do in the church before he can talk about the Spirit convicting the world (John 14–16). The movement of the Spirit is from God to the church and from the church to the outside world.

God acts in control of the nations   (verses 21–29)

Prediction is not the only part of prophecy. The prophet was as much a forthteller as a foreteller. But these chapters are full of prediction of the future and here God challenges false gods to predict the future (verses 22–26) and scorns the emptiness of their attempt. See also chapter 47:13 with its reminder of the folly of astrology, a lesson which needs to be learned again today. In our spiritual vacuum many people turn to astrology rather than theology. But God's view of the future is certain and does not depend on the position of the planets. God will prophesy the success of Cyrus who will bring the Jews out of exile. The Holy Spirit will announce things to come and Jesus promises in John 16:13 that he will guide us into all truth. It is on these grounds alone that we have confidence in our Lord's return and we are asked to watch for the signs of the times.

Cyrus is seen as being in God's hand. God not only predicts history, he also produces history. God can use a pagan ruler like Cyrus even though he is a great warrior on the march (verse 25). God is in charge although his ways are not always easy to understand as they unfold. Sometimes they are not easy to accept. But all other solutions are 'but wind and confusion' (verse 29). Not only does God know all things but he is also all-powerful, always working on behalf of his people and his own reputation in the world.

Questions

1. If we accept God as doing always what is right, in what way do we differ from unbiblical fatalists?
2. Prediction of the future is part of the prophetic role. Is this true of New Testament prophecy and if so what are the limits? Is there still valid prophecy today? If so, how important is it for our church?
3. Apply the poetic pictures of verses 17–20 to the practical realities of the spiritual life. Are you experiencing the truth of them?
4. Can you see God's hand at work in international affairs at the moment? How do you answer someone who says that the world is all out of control?

Isaiah 42:1–17

The gentle giant

The introduction of the 'servant of the Lord' is followed by a song of praise.

The words of verse 1 came as a word from heaven to Jesus (Matthew 3:17), a reminder of how important the Bible was to him. He will be ultimately the Servant and the picture of the servant begins to dominate the chapters to come. The phrase 'my servant' in 41:8 clearly refers to Israel, the nation, whereas here in verse 6 the servant has a ministry to Israel. The concept of the servant narrows from a nation to a remnant to a person and then begins to move out again through Jesus to the people of God and to the world. Verse 6 is similar to 49:6 which Paul quotes in relation to his own calling (Acts 13:47). In these verses the servant of God is also God at work. Only in Jesus is that combination fulfilled as seen in his action and teaching in John 13. In a manner beyond our understanding Jesus is both God and the servant of God at the same time.

The ministry of the servant

The servant comes in the first place to see justice established. The word justice is repeated three times in the first four verses. This is always a characteristic of God at work and is seen in God's king in chapters 11 and 32. But also liberty is proclaimed. Jesus quotes from Isaiah 61:1–2 in his famous Nazareth sermon on the same theme (Luke 4). Here in verse 7 there is a dynamic picture of true spiritual liberation. Jesus never released anyone from a literal prison in his ministry and indeed he allowed John the Baptist to languish in one. But there was much spiritual liberation and people released from many 'prisons' (see the story of the Gadarene demoniac in Mark 5). Justice and liberation go together.

This ministry will extend to a world united (verses 1–4) which will include the Gentiles (verse 6b). Simeon quotes these words when he welcomes the infant Jesus at the temple (Luke 2:32). Jesus comes to be the universal saviour and verses 11 and 12 are the trumpet call of a world rejoicing in the servant's activity.

The motivation of the servant

The Lord calls his servant to action: 'I am the Lord' (verse 8) and 'I, the LORD, have called' (verse 6). Once more God is working through his servant who is God himself at work. The servant is called by a covenant God (see next page). So in verse 1 he is described as 'my chosen one'. That will not only be true of Jesus but of all who follow in his service. So the servant will be called and strengthened by a creator God (see the song of verses 10–12). Indeed the creator God goes on doing new things (verses 8–9) so that here is a new song in verse 10. There is a sense of singing in these chapters (cf. 44:23). This must always be so when there is evidence of God at work.

The servant is also constantly sharing the character of a loving God. We have the tender picture of the Lord holding his hand (verse 6) contrasting with the rather violent pictures of God marching with the zeal of a warrior (verse 13), followed by the travail of a mother giving birth (verse 14). Love can also be very vulnerable. So Jesus spoke of the pain he endured when he went towards the cross (Luke 12:50) and Paul used the same metaphor of the pains of childbirth in Galatians 4:19. The tender picture of leading the blind (verse 16a) reminds us that his constant guidance will always be the strength of those who are fellow workers with him.

The marks of the servant

The first four verses of Isaiah 42 are quoted in Matthew 12:18–21 in relation to Jesus and his ministry being the fulfilment of Isaiah's prophecy. Gentleness is the theme in verses 2 and 3. Christian ministry needs to have that note of tenderness also (see 2 Timothy 2:24–26). But this does not deny the need to speak out boldly (cf. 40:3 and 9). That proclamation will not be self-advertising. The picture in verse 3 of being gentle to the bruised reed and the smouldering wick should always be an example to the people of God. Bold gentleness and gentle boldness should be our ideals.

Yet with that gentleness goes costliness and we need to remember the pain described in verse 14, albeit a productive pain ending in joy. With the costliness and the gentleness also goes mightiness. There is nothing weak about the ministry of the servant. The servant is a master and the master is the servant. The pathway is the way of the cross but that in itself is a message of power. It is significant in the Book of the Revelation that John sees the picture of the lamb who is a lion (Revelation 5:5–6) and the lamb who is a shepherd (Revelation 7:17). In between there is the picture of the wrath of the Lamb (Revelation 6:16). The servant is indeed a gentle giant.

Questions

1. Who then is this servant? How far can we see these verses as relevant to the world we all live in?
2. There is a promise here of new things and a new song. Is my church too opposed to change or too addicted to novelty?
3. The servant clearly has to learn to be silent and has to learn to speak. In which area do you most need to hear the challenge?

Bible covenant

Covenant is a most significant biblical word. The Old and New Testament technically mean the old and new covenants. It is God's promise to mankind and always has that one-sided emphasis. We must respond, but there is no bargain in God's covenant. It begins with the promise to Noah at the time of the Flood, continues with a very special promise to Abraham, is sealed at Sinai with Moses and then has the promise of a new covenant not written on stone (Jeremiah 31:31–34), but in the hearts of men and women. Jesus himself proclaimed that the new covenant had come when his blood was shed and that is remembered regularly at Holy Communion.

Here in Isaiah 42:6 and again in chapter 49:8 the Servant is seen as God's covenant person. He comes not only to fulfil God's covenant promise to David but also to institute the new covenant which would come about through his death. The significance of that new covenant is picked up in the letter to the Hebrews 8:6–13.

14

INCONSTANT SERVANTS AND UNCHANGING LORD
Isaiah 42:18 – 45:8

Isaiah 42:18 – 43:13

Witnesses to Jehovah

Israel has been both blind and deaf to God's approaches, yet they are to be God's witnesses to the word.

 The true witnesses of Jehovah (the LORD) are commissioned in chapter 43:10. For the Christian of today the New Testament equivalent is stated in Acts 1:8. Verse 11 here also reminds us of the great promises of Jesus with its words 'I am the Lord' (*cf.* John 14:6; 15:1; 6:35). There is a double note of witness in these verses. There is the witness or proof of God's love for us which continues however it is rebuffed (particularly see chapter 42:18–25). There is also the call for us to witness to him (43:10). The same double witness is found in John 15:26 and 27: the Holy Spirit testifies of God's love and we in turn testify to God through our lives.

The witness of God   (43:1–7)

The opening phrase 'But now' emphasizes that whatever happened in the past this is what God is saying now (*cf.* 44:1; 49:5 and Ephesians 2:13). God's love does not change but he is always ready to do something new. He loves us because he is our Creator and we are therefore related to him. This comes out in the opening two verses. God is sovereign over the world of creation, yet such a God wishes to have a personal relationship with his people, both as a nation and individually; hence the lovely promise at the end of verse 1 where we are called by name. The same idea is repeated in the relationship of the shepherd to his sheep in John 10:3. This relationship will survive the most testing circumstances and verse 2 gives us a promise of what will happen to his people in exile. They will be testing days but he will bring them through. Similarly Jesus promised that the gates of hell would not overcome against his church (Matthew 16:18).

God's love is seen not only in creation but in redemption; the phrase in the middle of verse 1 is important, 'I have redeemed you'. This idea is repeated in the great affirmation in verse 3a and again in verse 11. With the benefit of the New Testament we know that Jesus is the ultimate Saviour. The description of Christ's death as our ransom will be the glorious fulfilment of these promises. The liberation from exile described in verses 5–7 will be mirrored both in Christ's winning of a people to himself through the cross but also in the final gathering of the elect (Matthew 24:31). All of this will hinge on the great promise of verse 5, a constant refrain of Scripture: 'I am with you' (see p. 113). So God witnesses to his care and his love which will last for ever and will be seen in very practical terms.

The witness of man   (42:18–25 and 43:8–13)
Both by life and by lip the people of God are called to be witnesses. It is for that reason that God chose Israel in the Old Testament and chooses the church today. That community of people will always be frail and sinful (verse 8) and that is the tragic theme of chapter 42:18–25 where blind leaders of the blind failed in their ministry because they did not understand and they did not take the things of God to heart. Those searching verses were true in the day of our Lord concerning the Jewish nation. They are often true of the church of Jesus in any age. Yet twice in these verses God calls his people 'my witnesses' (verses 10 and 12). We are called to be witnesses to the unique nature of God (verse 11) and to his activity: he is a God who reveals, saves and proclaims (verse 12). That should be the content of our witness and wonderfully his witnesses are kept safe (verse 13).

The purpose of witness both here and in the New Testament is to let the world know the truth about God in the light of the blindness and deafness of society (verses 8–9). Our positive message is to bring people to know and believe in the person of our Lord (verse 10). So in the New Testament Jesus called his disciples to be with him and then sent them out. They were first disciples or learners and then apostles sent out with a message (*cf.* Mark 3:14–15).

Questions

1. Are there any ways in which the church can learn from those who style themselves Jehovah's Witnesses in our day? Amongst all the wrong things we know about them where do they challenge us?

2. Is the message of Christ having an impact on the wider world today? What do you know about the church in distant parts of the globe?

3. In what way does spiritual blindness and deafness show itself in our church today?

4. There is at the end of verse 1 a reminder of God's personal call by name. Reflect on how God calls you by name. What is your experience of that truth?

Isaiah 43:14–28

The gospel according to Isaiah

The elements of the New Testament gospel are revealed: God's mercy, our unfaithfulness and God's forgiveness.

Verse 25 anticipates the great New Testament gospel. It speaks of timeless truths concerning the character of God, linking with the 'I am' of verse 15. But this timeless God is always doing new things (verse 19, *cf.* Revelation 21:5). His immediate practical concern is Babylon (verse 14). But liberation from Babylon is a vivid picture of the freedom granted to the people of God from every kind of slavery.

The gospel of God's faithfulness   (verses 14–21)

God's faithfulness had been seen in the past in the rescue of his people at the Exodus (verses 16–17) and Paul, in 1 Corinthians 10:1–11, pointed out the spiritual significance of that event for the Christians of his day. God is always faithful to his people and his character is described in the great titles of verses 14 and 15 'Redeemer ... Holy One of Israel ... Creator ... King'. All these are aspects of the covenant name of the Lord (verse 15, see p. 120). The 'former things' spoken of in verse 18 refer to the Exodus. They are only to be remembered in the sense that they become a springboard for something new to happen. The people of God never dwell on the past although they learn from it.

Isaiah predicts that in the future there will be rescue from exile, promised in verse 14, the 'new thing' of verse 19. This is explained in pictorial language (verses 19–20) which has a timeless relevance. Behind every deliverance is a purpose which is to live and speak to the praise of God (verse 21: *cf.* 1 Peter 2:9).

The gospel of God's forgiveness   (verses 22–28)

At the heart of the gospel is the acknowledgment of sin, seen not only in acts of rebellion but in apathy and boredom towards God (see verses 22–23). Religion often becomes a wearisome nuisance when the heart of it is lost (see Malachi 1:13). God longs for people to bring offerings out of gratitude (verse 23) to the one who has born the burden of sin (verse 24). In our Lord's day much religion had lost its heart and become a burden (*cf.* Matthew 11:28–30). This had been a consistent pattern for the people of God (verses 26–27) even in the days of Abraham.

Verse 28 uses the language employed of Jericho, 'consigned to destruction', to Jerusalem itself (see Joshua 6:21). There is a grim possibility that even the house of God might be destroyed because of the rebellion of God's people. That sin needs to be acknowledged and forgiveness asked.

But alongside the need to acknowledge sin goes the promise of sin atoned. That is the beacon light of verse 25. The early Christian preacher Ambrose sent Augustine to this verse for peace of mind after his conversion experience. It speaks of God's eternal character and reminds us that God is not only the one who forgives, he is also the one who forgets. This lies behind the teaching of Jeremiah 31:34b and its fulfilment in Jesus' death and resurrection (see Colossians 2:13–15). Transgressions could only be blotted out because Jesus signed the new covenant in his blood. Isaiah is moving towards the hope of the Suffering Servant theme. We need to remember that the gospel we preach today had been long planned in the heart of the faithful, forgiving God.

Questions

1. Look at the titles of God in verses 14 and 15 and see how they still relate to the God of the New Testament. How far is the 'God of Israel' the God of the whole world?

2. In considering the possibility in verse 28 that Jerusalem could be destroyed, what does this say to us about our own church situation and how God judges it?

3. If God is a God who not only forgives but forgets, have you learned that lesson? In what ways does it challenge you?

Isaiah 44:1–23

A building project

The God of creation makes man in his image; foolish men make gods in their image, convenient but useless.

 There is a vivid contrast in construction designs in this chapter. In verses 12–20 there is an ironic description of the construction kit necessary for idol-making. Alongside it is the majestic picture of the Creator God, the great architect of the universe.

The Creator God   (verses 1–8, 21–24)

This chapter gives us a great view of God's unique person. Verses 6b and 8b remind us of the even greater vision in Revelation of the Alpha and the Omega, the Beginning and the End (Revelation 22:12). Isaiah has a strong concept of the one true God. God is still on the throne and the Creator God is also the Redeemer (verse 6a). He is the champion of his people and so he can proclaim through his prophet what is happening in history and announce future events (verse 7). Such a God brings calm, not fear, even in the midst of trouble (verse 8).

The more we know about God as a person the greater our insight into his plan; the master workman described in Proverbs 8:22–31 working through his servants (verses 1–2). Here Israel is seen as God's chosen servant and is given an affectionate name, Jeshurun (meaning the upright one). This name speaks of a close relationship (Deuteronomy 32:15) but it is one which can go sadly wrong (Deuteronomy 33:5). Through his servants God wishes to see the purpose of verse 5 being fulfilled. This is the picture of world mission. The conversion of the Gentiles which came to fruition in Acts is seen in embryo here. If that plan is to be fulfilled there is need for

God's provision. Verses 3 and 4 speak of the refreshing power of the Holy Spirit in the church and this anticipates the language used by Jesus himself (John 4:10–11 and 7:38–39). This is one of several Old Testament foreshadowings of Pentecost and its revolutionary fulfilment (see Ezekiel 36:26–27; Joel 2:28–29). There will be new fertility and fruitage when the Spirit comes and this will culminate in God's praise. The song of verse 23 comes from the remembrance of God's complete faithfulness (verse 21) and complete forgiveness (verse 22). All the universe delights in that message.

The created gods   (verses 9–20)

This scornful passage defies analysis. It demonstrates the absurdity of idolatry. *Things* cannot save us (*cf.* 40:18–20; 45:20; 46:1–7). In spite of the tolerant attitude of today there is no beauty in idols. They lead to tragedy and corruption. Idolatry is a mark of blindness which is often deliberate. Verse 18 is the key to the whole passage and should be compared with Romans 1:21 and 25. Men and women who are unwilling to face the truth about God prefer idols because they make no demands and allow for selfish worship.

The apostle John in 1 John 5:21 reminds us that idolatry continues in new, more sophisticated forms. It is vital to proclaim the one true God who alone can finally satisfy and who is still at work in his created world.

Questions

1. Isaiah has some very strong teaching about the one true God. Think of some of the implications of that doctrine on the way we think of the world.
2. Verse 3 refers to the refreshing ministry of the Holy Spirit. What does my church know of this reality?
3. List some modern idols. Where are you in danger of bowing the knee? Are you in any danger of treating God as an idol by making offerings to him and expecting him to do what you want?

Isaiah 44:24 – 45:8

God is still on the throne

God promises the return of Jerusalem's inhabitants by permission of King Cyrus.

 Cyrus appears for the first time by name in this passage nearly 200 years before the events that are described take place. He has been referred to in 41:2 and 25 by implication. His act of freeing the Jews from exile and allowing them to return and rebuild Jerusalem is reported in Ezra 1. World politics are seen to be under God's authority (a very important principle, see 10:5–6).

A meditation on sovereignty

God is seen in verse 24 as the Lord of creation with control over the large and the small. The one who made the heavens and the earth is still the one who forms the child in the womb (*cf.* Psalm 139). He is big enough for every eventuality and concerned about the smallest detail. God indeed has the tiny little baby in his hands as well as the whole wide world (*cf.* 40:10–12 where the mighty creator and the tender shepherd are one and the same person). It ought always to be true that genuine power goes along with genuine tenderness.

But God is also the Lord of history (verses 25–27). A Bible-believing person can never believe in the stars and fate: verses 24–25 indicate the unique authority of God who is not bound by man's ideas. Some years ago J.B. Phillips wrote a book entitled *Your God is too Small* (Epworth Press, 1952) and that title rings true for many of us. We have not only a God who acts in history but will interpret his actions and also predict the future. The reference in verses 26b–27 is to the return from exile. Outwardly, this will not be as majestic as the great miracle of the Exodus under Moses, but it demonstrates

129

God's triumph over every obstacle and leads to yet another occupa-
tion of the Promised Land. We have a God who can do old things
again but when he acts it is always a new thing.

God is also the Lord of everything (45:7–8). Verse 7 makes the
staggering claim that God is sovereign over darkness as well as
light, over disaster as well as prosperity. God never brings evil (*cf.*
James 1:13) but he can use evil for his purposes and turn the wrath
of man to his praise. Peter proclaimed that truth when he saw that
the cross, which demonstrates man's greatest rebellion and sin, can
become the agent of God's full salvation (Acts 2:33; 4:28). It was the
message that Job had to learn when everything went wrong in his
life (Job 2:10). Satan can work only as God allows him to, as the
prologue to the book of Job shows. In the book of the Revelation
Satan is often seen as being given authority for a specified period
but always under God's control. Everything finally works out for
salvation and righteousness (verse 8); such a claim demands a long
view of history. We need to beware of instant solutions and slick
prophesyings which are all the rage in a day when patience seems
to be a forgotten virtue.

An illustration of sovereignty

In chapters 44:28 and 45:1 we have a picture of Cyrus and some
remarkable words about his relationship to God '... my shepherd ...
his anointed ... whose right hand I take hold of'. These words will
be used of the Servant and our Lord himself. To Cyrus a very specific act of deliverance was entrusted, and because he, of all people,
was the agent of their freedom, the Jews had no reason to boast.
They did not plan their return from exile nor achieve it. Cyrus is a
tool in the hands of God. Probably to him the return of the Jews
was a very unimportant, trivial matter. But the biblical perspective
sees it differently. Often it is the small things of history which loom
large in the final analysis.

With this picture of the man goes the picture of the manner of his
work. In worldly eyes Cyrus was a very significant person and
God's act could have powerfully changed him. God calls him by
name and yet there is no apparent response from Cyrus (verses 4b
and 5b). In the record of Ezra 1:2–4 there does seem to be some
kind of acknowledgment of the God of Israel as the true God, but

no doubt to Cyrus there were many gods and there was no apparent personal acknowledgment of Jehovah, even though he was an instrument in God's hand. Whether leaders recognize him or not, God's objective is performed. His great concern is to bring glory to his name and bring people to acknowledge him (verses 5–6). This is a constant missionary incentive to the church with the added encouragement that God is already at work preparing the ground.

Questions
1. Can you think of any possible modern Cyrus being used by God to bring about his purpose, though not acknowledging him?
2. How can we keep the balance in our thinking and worship between the great Creator God and the tender caring God who formed us in the womb?
3. Think of chapter 45:7 and God's sovereignty over darkness. How can you interpret events in your life with this in mind?

15

GOD CARRIES
HIS PEOPLE
Isaiah 45:9 – 48:22

Isaiah 45:9–25

The potter's wheel

As the potter has total control over the creation of his pottery so God has total control over the creation of the universe and the events which occur in it.

 The potter is a familiar figure in the Bible (*cf.* 29:16 and Jeremiah 18). The potter's power of choice lies behind Paul's concept of divine election in Romans 9. In this section we find a beautiful contrast to the parody of idol-making in 44:12–20. The righteous of Isaiah's time and Christians today bow before the sovereign rights of the Creator. He makes careful plans in all he does, which is seen here in his dramatic use of King Cyrus.

The mind of the potter

The potter has total control over the concept, design and production of a piece of pottery and the clay has no say in the end result. This is also true of God in his creation. We see it in verses 18–25 where God is pictured as creator, revealer, saviour and king. In all these ways he is seen still to be carefully fashioning his people. Divine power has also divine purpose. God has salvation always in mind and verse 23 points to the fulfilment of this creative work which is seen by Paul to be fulfilled in Jesus (Philippians 2:10–11). Verses which refer in Isaiah to God the Father are translated in terms of God the Son in Paul's writings. This is a wonderful reminder of the overall biblical picture of the deity of Christ.

In order to fulfil this great purpose of salvation God uses Cyrus (verse 13) as he later called the apostle Paul to be his 'instrument' (Acts 9:15).

The miracle of the clay

In the divine potter's hand the passive clay becomes active. Men and women are made in the image of God but are responsible for their own actions. Therefore, the will of God's servant needs to be moulded. There is always the danger of rebellion against the potter's purposes (see the dramatic questions of verses 9 and 10). The mark of the true servant of God is to delight to do God's will, not just to do it reluctantly (see Psalm 40:8). Jesus made this clear when he taught his disciples how to pray: 'Our Father ... your will be done on earth as it is in heaven' (Matthew 6:10). In heaven God's will is done completely and joyfully. So often on earth it is done half-heartedly and reluctantly.

But everything depends upon the skill of the master. The potter's hands are the hands of the creator (verse 12). He can sometimes take us through painful processes but his ultimate aim is to make us fit to do his will on earth.

The importance of the vessel

The potter creates each pot for a particular purpose and each is important for the fulfilment of the role for which it is made. Paul uses the same picture in 2 Timothy 2 where he demonstrates that God chooses different people as his vessels to do his work; it is vital that those vessels, bearing God's hallmark, should be worthy of him. Ultimately this lies behind the Christian's concern for holiness of life. The potter chooses vessels (whether Cyrus [Isaiah 45] or Paul [Acts 9] or Christians today) to help to liberate God's people (verse 13). God may temporarily seem to be hiding himself (verse 15) but he is always at work even if we are not always aware of it. The book of Esther is a thrilling illustration of this truth. It is the only book in Scripture in which God's name never occurs, but there is no doubt about the activity of God keeping watch over his own and fulfilling his purposes.

But the scenario is more thrilling yet. It is not only the liberation of God's people but the extension of God's kingdom worldwide. Isaiah sees the whole world submitting to the people of God albeit very unwillingly (verse 14). Here is a reminder that God will have the final victory. In verse 22 there is a more positive note of salvation being accepted and enjoyed to the ends of the earth, for there is no other God and no other Saviour that can possibly bring about the divine purpose in the world. Ultimately, the potter will have his way.

Questions

1. These verses speak of the uniqueness of the true God as the only saviour. What does that say to us in terms of multi-faith services in our day?

2. Sometimes God seems to hide himself (verse 15). How do these verses help those in your church who may feel it to be true in their experience today?

3. Use the potter theme and work out where you may be grumbling at God's activity in your life at this moment.

Isaiah 46:1–13

Do we carry God or does he carry us?

The powerlessness of the idols of Babylon is compared with the power of the true God.

The contest between the power of idols and the power of the living God is a recurring theme throughout the Bible (see, for example, the account of Elijah and the prophets of Baal [1 Kings 18], the riot in Ephesus when Paul's teaching about Jesus clashed with the worship of Artemis [Acts 19] and John's command to 'keep yourselves from idols' [1 John 5:21]).

People love to make gods in their own image because they are convenient, but ultimately they become a burden. Isaiah points out that man-made gods, which literally have to be carried about, cannot support those who worship them. God is never a burden to us. On the contrary, he sustains us and promises to carry us (verse 4: *cf.* 63:9).

The god we carry

There is irony in this chapter with its description of the marauding troops under Cyrus carrying their gods with them. It is a philosophy of folly (verses 1–2) since dead idols cannot save but in fact become a burden. It is always folly to pray to a god who cannot save (45:20). Similarly the prophets of Baal shouted to their god in vain (1 Kings 18:26). It is also a philosophy of waste (verses 6–7). There is great extravagance here; nothing but the best went into their idols. Aaron too had built a golden calf which was very impressive in its luxury but absolutely ineffective (Exodus 32). False religion will always be costly without any benefit. It is tragic that so many people give generously to their idols, even in the cause of religion, but are deaf to the real needs of people. The genuine Christian gives and lives not so much to bolster up dead religion but to serve a living God who cares for people in their need.

Calling out for help to an object is ridiculed in verse 7. How can a response be obtained from a man-made object that cannot even move by itself, let alone answer? Idolaters are always whistling in the dark. Our Lord does not ask us to carry a dead-weight religion but offers instead a gospel of hope.

The God who carries us

The God of creation is described in verses 3 and 4: 'I have made you and I will carry you' gives us a wonderful stability and assurance. The creator God is committed to us because he has made us, a statement of particular value to those who, in the light of the New Testament, are born-again believers. Here too is the great I AM in verse 4 reminding us of the revelation to Moses (Exodus 3:14) and taken up by Jesus in the gospels.

The God of creation is also the God of providence (verse 5 and verses 8–11). He is not only the God of nature but the God of history and has proved himself in the life of his people Israel. He holds kings and nations in his hands. God's historic action brings great assurance to his people and the Christian faith is firmly based in the historic truth of the life, death and resurrection of Jesus.

The God of salvation appears again in verse 4b and verses 12 and 13. In these last verses words tumble over each other, offering deliverance and salvation, in the immediate context referring to the return from exile but applicable much more widely. The picture at the end of verse 4, in which God bears us up, links with 53:4 'he took up our infirmities and carried our sorrows'. The God who wants to carry us is the God who cared enough to send his Son all the way to Calvary. That is the heart of the gospel. We are not called to 'keep it up' but he is committed to keep us up, and this is the final assurance of the believer. Compared with the glorious gospel idolatry is not only sinful but utterly foolish.

Questions

1. Note the phrase in verse 4, 'I am he'. Think of some of the 'I am's' on the lips of Jesus which are relevant to a true understanding of our Saviour. Look at John 6:35; 8:58; 10:11; 11:25 and 14:6.
2. Idols demand an extravagant waste of money. How far do we waste money on foolish things in the life of our church?
3. How far are you trying to 'keep it up' in your progress as a Christian, rather than allowing him to keep you up? But is there also the danger of leaving it all to him?

Isaiah 47:1–15

Pride goes before destruction

Babylon is pictured as a proud queen/sorceress and her forthcoming fall is prophesied.

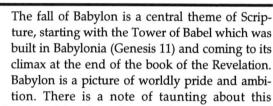 The fall of Babylon is a central theme of Scripture, starting with the Tower of Babel which was built in Babylonia (Genesis 11) and coming to its climax at the end of the book of the Revelation. Babylon is a picture of worldly pride and ambition. There is a note of taunting about this account, both in Isaiah and in other places, and yet also a note of sorrow. The sin of pride is always seen as ultimately subject to the sovereign hand of God who will not be mocked. In the midst of this grim chapter is a description of some of the wonderful names of God (verse 4).

The sin of pride

Babylon would be used against God's people, to fulfil the purposes of the sovereign God, but as a nation she alone was responsible for her acts. Like Assyria (10: 5–6) Babylon, the instrument in God's hands, would also suffer punishment because of her irresponsible actions and attitudes (*cf.* 42:24 and 43:28). Babylon was an arrogant nation and that is emphasized in the complacency and pride described in verse 7. One of the kings of Babylon, Nebuchadnezzar, expressed that arrogance in the proud language of Daniel 4:30 which led to immediate judgment and suffering. Here in verses 8 and 10 we read of the almost divine title used by Babylon and its king. Eventually totalitarian nations become like gods to be worshipped.

Once Babylon had been a most beautiful city and the description of 'queen of kingdoms' (verse 5) would have been true. But God's estimates are very different from ours. At the heart of this beautiful city was emptiness, and the magicians, the astrologers famous in Babylon, would have nothing to offer, hence the sarcasm in verse 12. The story of the book of Daniel demonstrates how feeble were the attempts of the astrologers of the day when matched with a word from the Lord (Daniel 2).

The certainty of punishment

The fate of Babylon is vividly described in poetic language which speaks of judgment without pity (verses 1–3). It is part of biblical truth that those who show no mercy receive no mercy. That is still true in New Testament teaching (cf. James 2:13). In this passage there is no unnecessary note of exultation even though Babylon had been the great enemy. Yet there is a sharp contrast between the description of Babylon's downfall (verse 1) and the description of the gaiety of Babylon in its heyday (verses 7–8). All too often when prosperity reigns and luxury is rampant people cannot conceive of the possibility of it all coming to an end.

When disaster comes there will be no help from magic (verse 13). The picture of the stubble being burnt up (verse 14) is also used in Malachi 4:1. We must always take seriously the solemnity of final judgment which is a constant theme in Scripture. Alongside that note of judgment is the tragedy referred to in verse 15 where the friends from days of prosperity are lost in days of disaster. It is foolish to build hopes on the permanence of worldly relationships.

Questions

1. Trace the fall of Babylon in Scripture and ponder what it says about the emptiness of worldly grandeur.
2. There are many references here to the inability of magic to do anything in the hour of need. What does this say about the interest in astrology in our day?
3. Pride is ultimately judged. How far are you in danger of that subtle sin?

Isaiah 48:1–22

Called by my name

The stubbornness of Israel is here described. Yet despite their shortcomings God promises to free his people and work through them.

 It is a privilege to bear the name of God. Israel had that privilege and yet it was a solemn responsibility. The people who were given that privilege and who bore that responsibility as they returned from exile were not a very promising lot, however. They sorely needed the teaching which begins at this point in the prophecy, the idea of the servant, applied to both people as a whole and also to a Person.

The people whom God will use   (verses 1–8)

God will use his own people who bear his name (Israel means 'he struggles with God': Genesis 32:28) in spite of their hypocrisy. Their pedigree is impeccable and they use the right words in worship, but there is no truth or righteousness in them (verse 1). Jesus repeats the same charge concerning the religious leaders of his day (Mark 7:6–7). It is always a danger to rely on using the right formula (verse 2) and this was solemnly pointed out by Amos (Amos 5:18). His people are unpromising material for our God to use, and yet he is able.

He would also use these people in spite of their hardness (verse 4). Throughout Scripture hardness of heart is seen as typical of mankind, for example, in the story of the Exodus Pharaoh continually hardened his heart (Exodus 7:13, 22 *etc.*) and it was a constant challenge in the New Testament (*e.g.* Mark 10:5; Hebrews 3:8). If we continue to harden our heart we may discover that it becomes set against the ways of God. We shall then be an easy prey for idolatry (verse 5).

God will use his people in spite of their rebellion. He promises to do a new thing as he brings them back from exile (verse 6b). But they need to remember that the rebellion of the past could happen again. Verse 8 is a constant refrain of history. There are things from which we should rebel in society and even in the church. But stubbornness towards God is a dangerous condition and it is easy to become proud of being rebellious. Remember, however, that God can change a Jacob into an Israel, a Simon into a Peter.

The purpose for which God will choose   (verses 9–22)

We see God calling (verse 12) and that word in Scripture does not only speak of the initial word of God to people but the assurance that he would carry his promise through to completion. In that sense every Christian is called.

It is a patient call. God is always longsuffering. His call is always completely unmerited (verse 9) and is done not merely for our sake but for his name's sake (verse 11). Because he cares about his name (his reputation) he delays his wrath, and he will work in us through the testing days (verse 10). The picture of the 'furnace of affliction' (verse 10) may remind us of the challenge of Daniel's day and the very real furnace through which Shadrach, Meshach and Abednego passed and found God in the heart of it (Daniel 3).

God's call is also painful to him. We do need to recollect that God makes himself vulnerable. There is pathos in the question in verse 11 (*cf.* Hosea 11:8) and in our Lord weeping over Jerusalem and saying 'How often would I ... but you would not'. Again in verse 17 there is a picture of parental care for the child with all the sadness of what might have been. Then come the tragic words of verse 22 (repeated in 57:21), 'There is no peace for the wicked'. That phrase, which has become a proverb in our language, is repeated in 57:21 and implied in 66:24.

But the call is a purposeful call. We are reminded yet again in verses 12–13 of God's unique person and the remarkable way in which he would use Cyrus (verses 14–16). Then comes the startling change of speaker (verse 16b). God has been speaking through Isaiah but now it is the servant beginning to speak through him (*cf.* 49:1; 50:4; 61:1). God is sovereign but we have a part to play: for example, the Jews are called to leave Babylon (verse 20: *cf.* 49:9 and 52:11). As they do, they will discover God's provision for the way (verse 21), rejoice in his power (verse 20) and enjoy his peace. The terms are still there for those whom God calls today.

Questions

1. 'No peace ... for the wicked.' What does that say about the way in which we can help to bring peace to our contemporary world?
2. The call to flee from Babylon is a challenge to have no compromise with worldly attitudes in the life of the church. How do we view this call in our church (for instance, in matters of leadership, finance, decision-making)?
3. This chapter is all about God's call. To what is he calling you today?

16

THE DAWN OF REDEMPTION
Isaiah 49:1–26

Isaiah 49:1–13

The day of salvation

The prophecy of God's Servant who will restore his people.

In the previous chapters the concept of the servant was identified with the nation of Israel but in this passage he is typified as a single person. In the New Testament Simeon quotes verse 6 to indicate that Isaiah's prophecy of the servant is being fulfilled in Jesus (Luke 3: 25–32). Paul and Barnabas also quote these words in relation to the gospel of Jesus Christ being spread to the Gentiles, bringing light and salvation (Acts 13:47). The prophecy of kings bowing before God's servant has echoes in the story of the wise men who worshipped the infant Jesus (Matthew 2:1–12) and the 'day of salvation' (verse 8) has become a reality in Jesus (2 Corinthians 6:2). These great truths hinge on the Servant of God whose ministry is eternal.

Seven hundred years after Isaiah's prophecy an Ethiopian chancellor was reading about the suffering Servant (Isaiah 53) and he asked Philip the Evangelist the question: '... who is the prophet talking about ...? '. Philip 'told him the good news of Jesus' (Acts 8:34–35). As we have seen above, the New Testament passages quoted identify Jesus with the Servant. In one sense he is Israel (verse 3 *cf.* 44:21) but in verse 5 the servant has a ministry to Israel so is obviously a single person, not a nation.

Who is the Servant?

There is no simple answer to the question but profound truths emerge in this chapter. For example, the call of the Servant includes a message for the whole world (verse 1) and it is rooted in the birth of the Servant (verse 1b). Jeremiah uses similar words to describe his call by God (Jeremiah 1:5) as does Paul (Galatians 1:15).

146

There comes a call to speak out in verse 2a (*cf.* 50:4–5 and Joshua 1:8). In that witness there will be divine protection where words are like an arrow concealed in God's quiver. There is great privilege for the Servant (verse 3a) because he is the trusted envoy, a word used of Moses (Exodus 14:31), of David (2 Samuel 3:18) and of the prophets (2 Kings 17:13). But with the privilege will come an increasing cost. This idea becomes clearer as we move towards the heart of the Suffering Servant passages. Here it is foreshadowed in the frustration described in verse 4 and rejection (verse 7). Not the least aspect of the cost is the apparent unpreparedness of people to listen.

But the Servant will ultimately conquer. The world will be at his feet (verse 7b) when the oppressors will finally acknowledge the sovereignty of God (*cf.* 60:14).

What will the Servant do?

In this passage the Servant's ministry is to Israel, physically to free them from exile and bring them home to Jerusalem (verse 5). But more importantly, in a spiritual sense his ministry is to free Israel from sin and restore them to their God. We meet the note of jubilee, the day of release, in verse 8 (*cf.* 61:1–2).

In a wider sense the Servant's ministry is seen to be to the whole world (verse 6) by means of the church. Paul states that salvation is for everyone who believes 'first for the Jew, then for the Gentile' (Romans 1:16) and after the rejection of his message by the Jewish community in Antioch he says 'We had to speak the word of God to you first. Since you reject it ... we now turn to the Gentiles ...' and he quotes Isaiah 49:6 to them (Acts 13:46–47). Before the world could be restored to its rightful God, the people of God must be renewed. So in the New Testament Jesus promises the Spirit, bringing revival and renewal to his church before the gospel can be preached to others.

The mission to bring salvation to the ends of the earth is the fulfilment of God's promise to Abraham (Genesis 12:1–3) which was renewed to Moses and the Israelites in the covenant at Sinai (Exodus 19:5–6).

The substance of the Servant's ministry is a message of freedom and peace. In verses 9 and 10 there is a lovely note of restoration which will be finally fulfilled only in the glorious picture of heaven in Revelation 7:16 and 17. In verses 9 and 10 there is a picture of Israel as sheep feeding by the roadside while God the shepherd guides them (verse 10), a recurrent theme (*cf.* 40:11).

With the message of peace there is also a message of power (verses 11–12). A powerful God turns the world upside-down (*cf.* 40:3–4) and brings back his people from every part of the world, hence the final note of joyful praise in verse 13.

Questions

1. The Servant is called to speak. How far is the church responsible for its guilty silence in a world of need?

2. Israel needs to be restored before the world can be won. Must our churches be renewed before we can tell the good news to the world outside? What sort of revival do we need and how would we recognize it?

3. The Servant would be conscious of God's hand upon him from birth. How far do you see that in your life?

Isaiah 49:14–26
A restored family

The prophecy switches from the person (Servant) to the place (Zion/Jerusalem) which will be restored.

In Bible history Jerusalem is always central. Here it is seen (verses 19–20) as desolate but hopeful of restoration. The key is in verse 23b with its suggestion of expectant waiting.

The current situation

The deserted city is vividly portrayed here, as it is in the book of Lamentations. In verse 14 it is described in the terms of a deserted woman. We are reminded of Jesus' words, quoting Psalm 22, as he hung on the cross. In verse 19 we read of a ruined city and in verses 24–26 comes a word to those who are prisoners and captives in a foreign land. Desertion and captivity are no strangers to modern life.

But there remains a devoted saviour for his people and the chapter ends with the lovely titles of God as Saviour, Redeemer and Mighty One of Jacob. There is a significant combination of strength and grace in those words. In verse 15 there is a mother picture of the heart of God (*cf.* 31:5). In verse 16 there is a further picture of God as the priest who brings the names of Israel on his hands in prayer (*cf.* Exodus 28:9–12).

Behind these loving pictures is the certainty of God's promises, hence the solemn oath of verse 18b. Once more we have the doctrine of the remnant with the words of the Sovereign Lord to undergird the truth (verses 22 and 25). God wants his name and power to be known (verse 23) and extended to all mankind (verse 26).

149

The future prospect

The Lord will bring back his people. In verse 17 the word 'son' might be translated as either 'sons' or 'builders', a picture that will be fulfilled in the rebuilding of the walls of Jerusalem by Nehemiah. In verse 18 it is prophesied that the Jews will return from exile but they also need to lift up their eyes beyond the present perspective. In a day of small things we too are to look to the horizon and see God at work. Isaiah can see the church (see next page) growing in exile (verses 20–21) and they will come back a renewed people. So in our world today it is often the persecuted church which grows and is more ready for renewal than the more apparently prosperous one. But God will always take up the cudgels on behalf of his own people (verse 25). The picture here is not only of the Lord bringing back but the church bursting out. Here is a reminder that the best days could be before us. That truth is expressed in verses 19–20 and reminds us of Zechariah 2 where the man with the measuring line is told not to confine the new Jerusalem to the limits of the old. In New Testament terms we have the picture of Gentiles being added to the flock as part of the heavenly Jerusalem (Galatians 4:25–27 cf. Isaiah 54:1). It all points to the final glory of heaven where the multitudes will be gathered together. So the prophet looks forward not only to the exile and restoration in the next century but to the continuing life of the church and the ultimate wonder of heaven.

There is a victory picture in verses 24–26. The exile had been necessary because of the sin of Israel which caused a breach in the relationship of his people with God (cf. 59:1–2). But God continues his work during their exile and promises a new exodus and redemption so that 'all mankind will know' (verse 26). The witness to the world is not only of individual conversion but of a corporate reality of God's blessing upon the church.

Questions

1. Jerusalem is very important in Scripture, both the earthly city and as a metaphor for heaven, but Christianity has no central place on earth. Does the church, as a body of people, in some way provide Christians with a centre?
2. The ideal of the church in these verses is of a growing family. How do we hold on to that picture without making single people feel excluded?

3. As you concentrate on 'small things', can you also see God at work in the wider world?
4. Verse 18 tells us to lift up our eyes. Are you guilty of not having a wide enough perspective of God's world and activity?

Isaiah, Israel and the church

We have often referred to Isaiah's vision of the church when he is writing of Israel, or 'the remnant' or the exiles. This is because the New Testament writers, and particularly Paul in the Letter to the Galatians, said that Isaiah's prophecy looked forward beyond the events of the Exile. The 'true Israel' will be those who follow Jesus Christ (see, for example, Galatians 3:29 and 6:16).

17

THE SUFFERING SERVANT CALLS HIS PEOPLE
Isaiah 50:1 – 52:12

Isaiah 50:1–11

The school of suffering

The Servant is described in terms of suffering persecution and violence.

The identity of the Servant begins to clarify and become more like Jesus. The events described in verse 6 are vividly fulfilled in the treatment given to Jesus (Mark 15:19) and verse 7 reminds us of Jesus' attitude as he set his face to Jerusalem (Luke 9:51).

The Servant's message

There is encouragement in the words of verses 1–3 with its reminder of the power of God still to save. There has been a tragic divorce between God and his people but it is not irrevocable. God has not sold his children to pay their debts. He is still faithful, but Israel has been fickle and the divorce was because of their sins (*cf.* Isaiah 59:1–2). As seen in the great drama of the book of Hosea, God keeps on loving even when his people turn their back upon him. Not only does he continue to love but he has the power to act and verses 2 and 3 continue the theme of the strength of God as creator; the God of creation and the God of providence.

The experience of the Servant will provide the content of his message and it will become a challenging word (verses 10 and 11). To the faithful there is great hope even in the midst of darkness. The way of trust and confidence will always win through. But there is also a challenge to the unbeliever (verse 11). Other religions and philosophies are fickle and give no lasting light. For those who have no time for God and his Servant there is a solemn warning of final torment which is a constant theme of Scripture and which we neglect to our peril. That message must be heard. To save us from that torment the ultimate Servant Jesus Christ, God's Son, died.

The Servant's ministry

The Servant would learn great lessons in the school of suffering and that idea is applied in Hebrews 5:8 to our Lord himself, a mystery beyond our understanding and calling for our worship. All the time we are getting nearer the Cross. The Servant has to learn to hear God before he can speak. Here is a picture of early morning vigils before God to receive the instruction 'morning by morning' (verse 4). That idea lies behind Jesus' words in the Lord's Prayer about our daily diet and the example he set in taking time by himself to pray. When the ear has been opened (verse 5) there is then an opportunity to open the lips. We must listen before we speak and listen more than we speak, but there remains a message to proclaim and we must not hold back. Samuel as a boy had to learn to say to God 'Speak, for your servant is listening' (1 Samuel 3:10), but then he was given the responsibility of passing on the message he had heard. The truth will come to us as we obey step by step.

Then in verse 6 we see the Servant responding to the persecution and he suffers martyrdom. This martyrdom theme is fulfilled in the gospels and repeated by Peter in 1 Peter 2:21–23, where he points to Jesus as an example to follow, accepting rather than seeking vengeance.

All of this is possible only because of the inward spirit being right with God and making a right response to opposition and persecution. Always the Servant is aware of the sovereign Lord, as was Jesus as he went to Calvary. But the awareness of the Lord's help (verses 7a and 9a) still calls for a personal dedication (verse 7b). There is the assurance of final vindication: ultimately the Servant will not be put to shame. Paul picks up this theme in Romans 8:31–39 with a far greater assurance because Calvary is past and the resurrection has happened. Even though suffering comes, there is final triumph. At the end of the school of suffering there is a glorious graduation day.

Questions

1. Meditate on the Servant's likeness to Jesus and marvel at the cost of his sacrifice for the world.
2. How much should there be an experience of the cross in the life of your church and what does that mean in practical terms?
3. There is the promise for the servant that God speaks morning by morning. What are you learning about the value of making time, particularly early in the day, to be with your Lord?

Isaiah 51:1–16

A song for the road

God reminds his people that he has always looked after them. Isaiah then calls upon God to act once more and restore them again.

Even in this section on the Suffering Servant there is the sound of singing (verse 3) and the promise of return from exile singing (verse 11). Doubts about God have become for his people doubts about themselves but here is a chapter to encourage. The song will be a marching song but before the sound of singing comes the sound of silence.

Listen! (verses 1–8)

The Bible insists that 'faith comes by hearing, and hearing by the word of God' (Romans 10:17 AV). Three times we are called to 'Listen to me' (verses 1, 4, 7). The first three verses encourage hope by looking at the past. In days of depression it is often good to look back, not least to biblical history. Here is the example of Abraham and what God could do with one man of consistent faith. In verse 2 there is a clear contrast between the one and the many. God can use the smallest nucleus as Jesus illustrated in the parable of the mustard seed (Luke 13:18–19), and the amazing story of Pentecost (Acts 2:1–11). But this growth is only for those who actively pursue God's way and seek the Lord as a priority. These are the people who will look in the right direction, 'to the heavens', or look only earthwards (verse 6). For such, in the worst days of barrenness, there comes hope (verse 3).

Hope also looks to the future, although this seems to be very distant (verse 6), words echoed in 2 Peter 3:10 and paralleled with our

Lord's words in Mark 13:31. There Jesus promises that even though the very universe disintegrates his word remains valid. Not only does Christ's word live for ever but this verse reminds us that God's salvation and righteousness will also remain for ever. That ultimate hope leads to the immediate hope expressed in verses 4 and 5 where God will act in justice and righteousness restoring Israel. That restoration leads them on again to 'the nations'. This book is a missionary document in embryo!

In verses 7 and 8, hope is anchored in the present. The people of God often look so weak and insignificant and yet with God on their side they are always a strong majority. Never despise the day of 'small things' (Zechariah 4:10).

Wake up! (verses 9–16)

Jerusalem will be called to wake up (verse 17; 52:1), but here God is called to awake! In verses 9–11 the strength of God's hand is remembered. Rahab is a reference to Egypt (see 30:7 and Psalm 87:4) and the sea-monster a symbol of Egypt, so here is another reminder of the miracle of the Exodus which was 'the day of God's right hand' (cf. Exodus 15:6, 11 and 12). Here in verse 11 is the promise of another exodus with the same God at work and the same cause for rejoicing (cf. Psalm 126).

In a wonderful way, God's strong right hand is also a protecting hand and here it is seen as a shade for his people (verses 12–16). There is a note of safety, protection and peace. It is the work of God the creator and the one who keeps his covenant. Why should the Israelites be so fearful of 'mortal men', 'live in constant terror every day' (verses 12 and 13) and forget 'the LORD your Maker', when he will protect them 'with the shadow of my hand' (verse 16)?

The climax comes in verse 16 with the picture of the whole of the people of God seen as a servant called to proclaim the words of God. There is significance in the order of the words in this verse, 'heavens ... earth ... Zion': the God who made the heavens and the earth cares for his people. The last phrase is the great assurance of the church at every stage: 'You are my people' – here is our hope. This is the essence of our song, that we are safe in the shadow of his hand.

Questions

1. Singing has an important place in Scripture and in the Christian community. What are the dangers of false triumphalism (that is, an attitude of self-righteous pride)?
2. The missionary vision keeps recurring in Isaiah. How far does your church look beyond its own frontiers in prayer and servce? How can we serve the wider world?
3. Verse 16 speaks of protection at all times for the people of God. In what way do you need to claim that promise today?

Isaiah 51:17 – 52:12

A tale of two cities – part 2

As in chapter 2 there is a vivid contrast between the ideal and the real city of Jerusalem. One was seen as lying in ruins, the other to be restored.

 God's wrath has fallen on Jerusalem and 'double calamities' have come on the city. But God will restore his city and redeem his people and there will be a new heavenly city, Zion.

A city destroyed   (51:17–23)

Judgment is experienced by the people of God and is described with vivid picture-language: a blind woman groping in the dark (verse 18) and a deer trapped and unable to escape (verse 20). More literally there is a picture of young men fainting on the ground at the head of every street (verse 20: *cf.* Lamentations 2:11–12). It is easy to see in this picture the present reality of many cities in our modern world. Isaiah sees this kind of destruction as the result of God's wrath (verse 20b) and in terms of a cup to be drunk (verse 17). Our Lord used the same picture during the last supper when he used the cup as a symbol of his blood being shed in a new covenant (Matthew 26:27–28), and when he prayed to God the night before his death on the cross: the supreme evidence not only of God's love but of God's wrath (Matthew 26:39, 42; Mark 14:36; Luke 22:42).

This judgment will be extended to others (verses 21–23). There will be the destruction of Babylon as well as the restoration of Jerusalem. Those who humiliate God's people will not go unpunished. In the plan of God, Jesus himself would drink the cup of judgment to the last dregs. No-one else may have to drink that much, but there will be those who reject him who will certainly themselves drink from that cup of wrath.

A city celebrating (52:1–12)

Using the illustration of buying a slave out of slavery, a common event in his day, Isaiah pictures the people of Israel, 'Daughter of Zion', redeemed from their literal and spiritual slavery. They are not redeemed by money but by the Lord, the Redeemer (48:17; 49:26). In the New Testament Jesus is the fulfilment of the Redeemer in his death and resurrection (1 Peter 1:18–19; Mark 10:45). Dishonour had been brought to God's name, hence the judgment (51:5–6). The restoration of God's people will also be because of God's name and his concern that it should be honoured (*cf.* Ezekiel 36:21–22). That is why there is a call to God's people to wake up so that Jerusalem might worthily represent their Lord (verses 1–2).

The redeemed people should also be a rejoicing people. Verses 7–10 give us a chorus of great beauty in the dawning hope of restoration. It is the message of the watchman, which is common in Scripture, as he waits both for signs of judgment and of hope. Here is the clarion call of a renewed people and above all of the activity of God demonstrated in it. The refrain, 'Your God reigns' is a timeless cry. It is a message for the whole world (verse 10: *cf.* Psalm 98:3–4). Meantime even the ruins are urged to 'sing for joy' (verse 9). We do not have to wait for the final fulfilment to enjoy this message; God's people are renewed as well as redeemed and rejoicing. There is a thoughtful ending to this wonderful passage in verses 11 and 12. There is always a price to pay for liberty and here is the call to pull out of Babylon when the opportunity comes and to be renewed in a life of holiness. There will be a literal journey for those who come out of Babylon (Ezra 1:5–11) and for the journey the promise that God will go with them as he did in the Exodus (verse 12: *cf.* Exodus 13:21). For us today there is a challenge to be willing to be separated from all that is worldly and unworthy of the people of God (verse 11: *cf.* 2 Corinthians 6:17). Verse 11 hints at a priestly procession. In the New Testament picture of the priesthood of all believers, we are all meant to live this life of pure cleanliness.

Questions

1. Cities clearly matter in God's strategy. What are some of the implications of evangelizing vast cities today?

2. Look at the word-picture of the cup as it is fulfilled in the New Testament. Compare Matthew 26 verses 26–29 with verses 39–42. How far does this lead to a new sense of thankfulness in the life of the church?

3. If we are all now part of the priesthood of all believers, what does verse 11 say to you about your responsibility for holiness of life?

18

SALVATION
PROCLAIMED
Isaiah 52:13 – 55:13

Isaiah 52:13 – 53:12
The glory of the cross

In this chapter, the Servant is revealed as the One who will suffer on behalf of God's people and will bear their sins.

 The cross, the central pivot of all history, casts its light in every direction. In the Old Testament it shines in many places but none more clearly than this remarkable chapter 53. The solitary figure here can only finally mean Jesus, the interpretation that Philip made when speaking to the Ethiopian Chancellor (Acts 8). Isaiah 53 is the most quoted of Old Testament chapters in the New Testament, being the inspiration of 1 Peter 2 and even our Lord's own words in Mark 10:45. In the NIV translation it is a beautifully symmetrical chapter with five paragraphs of three verses each, with God and man speaking alternately.

A surprising Saviour   (52: 13–15)
So far the word 'exalted' has been used of God the Father (6:1; 5:16 and 33:5). Here it is used of the Servant, and will be so used in the New Testament in Acts 2:33 and Philippians 2:9, clearly referring to Jesus Christ. It is linked with the word 'lifted up' which Jesus uses about his own work on the cross (John 3:14; 8:28). Verse 14 fits that moment when Jesus was led out by Pilate to the crowds and the Roman Governor said 'Here is the man' (John 19:5).

A rejected Saviour   (53: 1–3)
The book of Isaiah is full of wonderfully descriptive passages and this one depicting the Suffering Servant is one of the most beautiful. There is no triumphalism in this passage, only a glimpse of

what Jesus really had to suffer on the cross, 'despised and rejected of men'. This is such a familiar passage that it warrants careful reading, perhaps using two or three different translations of the Bible to give us fresh insight into it.

There is nothing obviously attractive about the Jesus of Calvary nor does he strike an impressive figure. His ministry and death are characterized more by suffering than by power, and salvation through the cross will always appear foolish to the people of this world (1 Corinthians 1:20–24).

A representative Saviour   (53:4–6)

Here is the great theme of suffering on our behalf which Paul takes up in 2 Corinthians 5:21: the words 'he' and 'we' are emphatic. The pain of Calvary described in verses 4–5 was more than physical. There was mental and spiritual agony both in the Garden of Gethsemane and on the cross as Jesus drank God's cup of wrath. Yet this became the place of our salvation. The great theme of Scripture, which had begun with the idea of the goat of the Old Testament on whose head the penitent laid his or her hand, was being fulfilled (Leviticus 16:21). The theme abounds in the New Testament (see 1 Corinthians 6:20; 1 Peter 1:18–19; Revelation 7:14). The verbs used in verse 5 are full of poignancy. The word 'pierced' has echoes of Psalm 22:16 and Zechariah 12:10 and is seen as fulfilled at the cross (John 19:34). He was crushed in spiritual terms and yet that burden of sin resting upon Christ meant liberation for us. The great message of Calvary is 'Christ for us'. The three great themes of the Christian Festivals need to be balanced. Christmas is God with us; Easter is God for us and Pentecost is God in us.

A suffering Saviour   (53:7–9)

There is nothing neatly theological here. Rather we are faced with human suffering at a deep level. The servant is likened to a lamb being led to slaughter, powerless and unable to speak, a picture also used by Jeremiah of himself (Jeremiah 11:19). There are many similarities between Jeremiah and Jesus, but with Jesus there is no spirit of vengeance and this impressed Peter enormously (1 Peter 2:23–24).

There was a remarkable fulfilment of verse 9 when Jesus unexpectedly found a resting place in the tomb of Joseph of Arimathea.

165

The whole episode of the trials and crucifixion of Jesus was hideously unfair and yet it was the deliberate and willing act of the Lamb of God (John 12:27–28).

A sovereign Saviour   (53:10–12)

The persecutors fade away and the Lord and the Servant dominate. God is in control, reconciling the world to himself (*cf.* Acts 4:28).

There is a wonderful mix of divine sovereignty and human choice here. 'It was the Lord's will' (verse 10) and yet the Servant 'poured out his life unto death' (verse 12). There are many pictures of the saving work of the Servant here – the sacrificial offering (verse 10), justification (verse 11), identification with sinners (verse 12). Yet there will be a final triumph. The suffering is like the birth pangs which bring in a new age (verse 11). There is no place in the Old Testament where we are nearer to the heart of the gospel than here.

Questions
1. Follow the New Testament links of this remarkable passage, referred to above, and spend time in profound praise.
2. Consider the teaching and worship of your church. How far is it centred on the cross?
3. The word 'exalted' means 'lifted up'. It speaks of the cross and the ascension. What does it say to you about your expectations in following the footsteps of Jesus?

Isaiah 54:1–17

Expect great things

Isaiah looks forward to the time when Jerusalem will rejoice like a previously childless woman who has received the gift of children. God's people should expect undreamed-of future glories.

The historic Jerusalem is seen as a prototype of the heavenly Jerusalem which Paul calls 'our mother' (Galatians 4:26). This chapter, 54, speaking of the growing church, comes after chapter 53 with its stress on the death of the Servant, and before chapter 55 with its gospel call. This is the pattern for the New Testament and it is not surprising that this chapter is quoted in it (Galatians 4; Revelation 21). There are two pictures of the church: the family of God and the city of God, a community growing in love as well as in numbers.

The family of God   (verses 1–10)

Isaiah begins by referring to three situations affecting women, which in Old Testament times and even today are a stigma and source of humiliation. They are symbolic of the state that Israel is in. He starts with the tragedy of barrenness which in Old Testament days was a grim reality. The stories of Sarah (Genesis 16, 18) and Hannah (1 Samuel 1) remind us of this. In verse 4, the picture is of widowhood which again spoke volumes in Old Testament days when the widow was left without any financial resources. In verses 5–7, Jerusalem is seen as a deserted wife (who again would be left without resources) who has been abandoned by God. God's love does not change, but it is jealous love and the history of Israel has demonstrated the folly of rejecting that love. Verse 4 speaks of 'the shame of your youth' with reference to the Jews in slavery in Egypt and now in exile in Babylon.

There is also here a picture of restoration which is the chief theme of the chapter. That is why it opens with a call to sing in verse 1. Singing is always a demonstration of God at work, hence the Jews could not sing in exile when they were away from the Lord's land (Psalm 137). The reason for singing is that Israel will have many more children than Babylon (verse 1b, a picture of God's favour). She may sing in anticipation of glories to come. In verse 2 we have a picture of a world mission, both in depth and breadth. To cope with the huge increase of numbers the cords are to be lengthened and stakes strengthened in the tent, which typifies the church of God (*cf.* 33:20). In verse 3 there is a clear promise of the expansion of the people of God: it all stems from the work of God who is pictured as 'husband and redeemer' and the Holy One of Israel (verse 5). There is no conflict in Scripture between the love and the holiness of God. In verses 7 and 8 his holy love is depicted as deep compassion and everlasting kindness. God keeps his covenant (his agreement with Israel) from the day of Noah onwards and that covenant is 'my covenant of peace' (verse 10). For us who live on this side of Calvary we know this is the New Covenant promised by Jeremiah and fulfilled at the cross. Such a covenant is more enduring than the created universe itself (verse 10).

The city of God   (verses 11–17)

It seems a long way from the tent of verse 2 to the gorgeous city of verses 11 and 12, just as there is a great contrast between the earthly church and the heavenly Jerusalem. True beauty is to be found in the virtues of peace and righteousness and a true relationship with the Lord (verses 13–14). Ultimately this promise of glory will be fulfilled only in the heavenly kingdom but it is to be seen on earth within a family where people are reconciled to God and to one another.

With the beauty also goes God's impregnable strength (verses 14–17). There is no promise of immunity from attack, but the final triumph of the truth is assured. God can use evil forces to bring his people to their knees in repentance and he does have the last word (verse 16). It is significant that this is a promise for 'the servants of the Lord' (verse 17). We have seen much of the ministry of the Servant; now it is for the servants who will benefit from the Servant's ministry. Here only, in the City of God, is security and the assurance of final salvation. We are reminded of the ark of Noah (verse 9). From that kind of security there will be a great desire to share the gospel with others, a preparation for the invitation in chapter 55.

Questions

1. Verse 2 speaks of both breadth and depth in the church. What does that mean in terms of the balance between teaching and evangelism?
2. There are pictures of beauty in the church here. Looking at your church what does 'beauty' signify?
3. Note the references to peace and security in these verses and apply them to the temptations to the opposite in your own life.
4. Can political, economic and social endeavours help in any way to prepare for the heavenly Jerusalem or are all such efforts a waste of time and energy?

Isaiah 55:1–13

The gospel invitation

A chapter full of pictures of God's gracious invitation to the thirsty and the wrongdoer and the depths and heights of his forgiving mercy.

 This chapter contains one of the great invitations in Scripture and can be compared with our Lord's moving words in Matthew 11:28–29. There is a great warmth of welcome starting with the four-fold 'come' in verse 1 similar to that which ends Scripture in Revelation 22:17.

There are two distinct halves to the invitation. People are seen as hungry needing satisfaction, and as wicked needing salvation. There is no short cut to the first without the reality of the second.

Welcome to the needy   (verses 1–5)

The needy person is seen as unsatisfied, like the woman at the well (John 4) and those invited to drink by Jesus (John 7:37). There is tragedy in missing true satisfaction by being content with something less than is offered. This happened when the Jewish people preferred the mirage to the true oasis of satisfaction (Jeremiah 2:13). These verses remind us that God's gift is of grace and cannot be earned: it can only be a free gift for us because the price has already been paid. Isaiah 55 would not be true apart from the truth of Isaiah 53 (*cf.* Mark 10:45 and Romans 6:23). We have here not just a basic offer but the promise of abundant life with wine and milk as in our Lord's words with their promise of abundant life (John 10:10).

The offer in verses 2–3 speaks of salvation. It is possible to be satisfied with the husks of pagan religion (implied in verse 2) as was

170

true of the prodigal, feeding on pigs' food until he came to his senses (Luke 15). He too was invited back to a banquet, and that theme appears frequently in our Lord's parables as well as here (verse 2b). God's invitation is called 'an everlasting covenant' (verse 3) and is linked back to the promise to David in 2 Samuel 7:14–17. This verse is quoted in Acts 13:34 in the context of the resurrection of Jesus, the one greater than David. The promise of our Lord remains and we live now in the light of the New Covenant.

The satisfaction offered should never be selfishly enjoyed. Verses 4 and 5 are a call to overflow in witness to others (see also John 7:37–38; Acts 1:8). Here is the promise of a world seeking after the Lord, which will be gloriously fulfilled as recorded in the Acts of the Apostles. We cannot, however, offer to others what we have not first fully received and enjoyed ourselves.

Welcome to the sinner (verses 6–13)

Verses 6 and 7 speak of the entry to the Lord's presence in similar language to that used by Jesus when he speaks of himself as the door (John 10:7, 9 AV). There is always a note of repentance at the heart of Christian experience. In verse 7 there is a classic statement of the way into the Kingdom. It refers to the mind rather than the emotions and it is a call to the will with its commands to 'forsake' and 'turn to the LORD'. It deals with habits and ways and thoughts and not just feelings: Paul sums this up in Romans 6:17 with his definition of the response to the gospel, obedience. There is a negative aspect and a positive one (turn away from evil and turn to the Lord) and both are seen as a personal response to the Lord, with a cry for mercy and pardon. This great verse conveys the confidence that God is only too ready to pardon those who come in repentance but there is in verse 6 the note of urgency. It would be tragic to miss the blessing because we delayed in seeking it.

Verses 8–13 speak of the way forward. There is a promise that those who seek will find (cf. Jeremiah 29:13–14 and Matthew 7:7–8). So verses 8 and 9 here underline the promise of mercy and pardon in verse 7. God never fails, and his offer is always beyond our expectation. Verses 10–13 poetically describe the blessing offered to those who come and accept the invitation. The rain and the snow suggest a transformation depending upon the power of God's

Word (verse 10). Hebrews 4:12 reminds us that God's Word cuts both ways and his purposes will include judgment as well as liberation.

The final promise is one of joyful liberty (verse 12) and fruitfulness (verse 13). Here is a reversal of the curse of Eden (Genesis 3:17–19) which is a great theme of Scripture. It comes to us as a reminder of a free offer. It was costly for God to give it and there is a cost in receiving it, but there is a greater cost in rejection. He paid the price that we might enjoy the free offer. 'O Lamb of God I come.'

Questions

1. This chapter speaks of the power of the Word of God. Consider what that says about the centrality of Scripture in the life of the church and the believer.
2. Verse 7 sums up true evangelistic preaching. How does your church relate to this kind of preaching?
3. There is a promise here of an abundant supply. Are you too often content with just the basics?
4. The world outside the church does not seem to understand the Lord's loving invitation to free salvation. What is needed for this to happen?

 ## Liberation theology

Down the centuries Christians have been associated with many movements of social and political liberation. It was evangelical leadership which helped to abolish slavery in the western world in the nineteenth century. In our modern age many movements in totalitarian countries have had Christian support in bringing democracy to those without the vote and in improving social conditions for those living in grim conditions. There is always a danger that political and social action becomes a substitute for the gospel which brings liberation from sin. Clearly the letter of James reminds us that unless there is social care the preaching of the gospel is invalid. But social activity alone is not sufficient for salvation.

This theme is highlighted in our Lord's use of Isaiah 61:1–2 when he preached at Nazareth (Luke 4:16–30). Although he spoke of proclaiming freedom for the captives there was a significant figure in prison in the person of John the Baptist and Jesus did nothing to release him. Obviously he was speaking in spiritual terms, just as he did when he debated with religious leaders about the meaning of slavery and freedom (John 8:31–36). He claimed that whoever sins is a slave to sin while his opponents were arguing that they had never been slaves as the people of God. Their memories were clearly short but they were talking at a different level. For Jesus, freedom meant freedom from the bondage of sin and in every society this must be the first priority. Liberation theology focuses on social change as the first priority.

If evangelical Christians had always been concerned about the social implications of the gospel perhaps there would not have been the tension there is today between the liberation theology which bypasses the cross and evangelistic preaching which sometimes ignores the social deprivation of our day.

19

THE SHAME OF GOD'S CHOSEN PEOPLE
Isaiah 56:1 – 59:21

Isaiah 56:1–12
Double vision

The Lord calls his people to live well in the light of their salvation, but their leaders are setting a poor example.

 Isaiah ends his book with beautiful symmetry. Chapters 60 to 62 form a magnificent description of restored Jerusalem. Around them are grim chapters of corruption (57 to 59) and devastation (63 to 64). On either side of these chapters is a picture of a people ready to reach out to others in God's name and yet often with deep division within their own community. It is the story of Judaism and its tragedy; it is often the story of the church too; the glory and the shame.

Vision clear   (verses 1–8)

We are brought down to earth after the gospel invitation of chapter 55. Proof of response to that message must be seen in a life of consistency, caring about justice and being ready to put things right. One particular aspect of this response will be seen in the people's attitude to the Sabbath day which is seen in verse 2 as a mark of loyalty as well as a way of health. This will become the theme of chapter 58. We need to recollect that similar principles apply to our Lord's day even though there is a dynamism about it which is greater than mere Sabbath observance.

The alien is to be welcomed (verse 3). This is a vision of outreach never lost completely in the Old Testament, but tragically it was forgotten at many periods in Israel's history as it has been even more sadly in our own church history. Outreach, however, could be perverted in a spirit of over-zealous recruitment condemned by our Lord in Matthew 23:15. The concern for the eunuch (verses 3–5) would be very significant after return from Babylon where many would have suffered sexual mutilation in this way. There is a promise in verse 5 to those who have no family of their own, to discover another family. This is significant in the light of the New Testament concept of the body of Christ, the church.

In the Lord's service and worship there is to be unity across all nationalities (verses 6–8). This is highlighted in the concept of the temple being seen as 'the house of prayer for all nations' (verse 7). Our Lord himself in cleansing the temple protested strongly that this vision had been lost and it had become instead a den of thieves (*cf.* Matthew 21:13). Then in verse 8 we have the foreshadowing of our Lord's words describing himself as the good shepherd of the one flock (John 10:16).

Vision clouded   (verses 9–12)

In these closing verses there are two pictures with a similar message describing the bankrupt leadership of the nation and the church of Isaiah's age, a message which all too often applies also to our own generation. The watchmen had gone to sleep. The result was the devastation of verse 9 and the terrible condemnation of verse 10. Here are leaders with no vision, no message, escapist and self-pleasing – drunk dogs, sleeping dogs, greedy dogs. This call to watchmen is repeated in Isaiah (*cf.* 52:8 and 62:6) and it is a constant theme in Ezekiel (*cf.* 3:17). It comes as a challenge to the watchful, prayerful life of every believer within the church but with special reference to those called to leadership.

The other comparison in verses 11b–12 is that of the shepherd, given a new dimension by our Lord in his teaching (John 10). Here the shepherd who should be tending the flock is looking after himself (verse 12). There could be no restored Jerusalem without renewed leadership and such renewal remains an urgent concern for our day.

We need to pray for good shepherds and faithful watchmen.

Questions

1. There is a hint here about the tragedy of sexual abuse (verse 3b). How do we try to minister to victims in our day?
2. The vision of the temple as a house of prayer for everyone should lie behind our thinking about our church. How do we feel in this respect? Are some people more welcome than others?
3. What does the call to be faithful as watchmen say about the consistency of your own prayer life?

Sabbath

This comes from a Hebrew verb which means 'to cease'. As such, it comes in Genesis 2:2 with a reference to God ceasing from his work of creation. So the concept of one day in seven different from the rest is a 'creation ordinance' and is meant for the good of men and women whatever their belief. But it has special significance for the people of the Old Testament as marking God's deliverances. So in Exodus 20:8–11 it marks the Exodus from Egypt and the Sabbath is seen as a sign of the covenant with Moses. Twice in Exodus this note is repeated – in chapter 16 with the giving of the manna where there was to be no collection of God's gift on the Sabbath, and in chapter 31:12–17 where there is renewed emphasis on the Sabbath at the time of the building of the Tabernacle.

When the deliverance from exile would happen the Sabbath would again be a mark of thanksgiving. This is the theme of chapter 56:6, repeated in 58:13 and 66:23.

In the New Testament the Lord's Day becomes the new Sabbath for Christians. On that day is celebrated the greatest deliverance of all, the resurrection of Jesus. So it becomes a time for Christian worship (Acts 20:7), when Christians bring their gifts in fellowship (1 Corinthians 16:2) and when John had his vision on the Island of Patmos 'in the Spirit on the Lord's Day' (Revelation 1:10).

Jesus argued against a legalistic Sabbath where the rules and regulations had become ludicrous. He was law-abiding and he worshipped on the Sabbath, but he called himself Lord of the Sabbath (Mark 2:28) and deliberately healed people on the Sabbath Day as a mark that this was a day of God's continued activity in mercy and love.

Isaiah 57:1–21

No peace for the wicked

Another chapter of contrast: between the folly of idolatry and the comfort offered to those who come humbly to God.

 'No peace for the wicked' has become a familiar and superficial proverb. Here it is a grim reality. It contrasts with the peace offered in verses 2 and 19. There is tragedy in the restlessness of the wicked (verse 20) because they have rejected God's way of peace.

At war with God (verses 1–13)

Because of the rejection of God's ways the floodgates of sin are now seen to be open. The climax will come in the terrible days of Manasseh whose life is briefly recorded in 2 Kings 21:1–17 (see especially verses 6 and 16). His supreme sin was the sacrifice of his son to the idol of Molech. This event was prophesied here in verses 5b and 9. It would be better to die than to have to face those days. That seems to be the sentiment behind the language of verse 2.

That age would merge sexual immorality with religious idolatry. Very often these two go together. True religion will be mocked (verse 4: *cf.* 28:9 and 14) and idolatry will be rampant. Idolatry is always easier than faith in the true God because it makes no moral demands. Man-made gods cannot do anything, nor do they demand anything.

This way of wickedness will eventually lead to the weariness described in verse 10. Sin does not satisfy and yet there is no turning back. Disillusionment often leads to further disobedience rather than to repentance. In our Lord's story of the Prodigal Son the son does not immediately turn back to his father when he is in the

179

depths of despair. He goes even further down until he can go no further and then he comes to his senses.

At peace with God   (verses 14–21)

These verses describe the triumph of grace. It is the offer of a great God who condescends to care for lowly people on the assumption that their response will be one of penitence. The word 'contrite' has the note of being crushed or broken. This vision of the high and lofty God fits perfectly with the vision which sent Isaiah on his way (6:1) and also with the picture of the Suffering Servant in chapter 52:13.

The righteous anger of God goes alongside a readiness to heal and guide (see verses 18 and 19). True peace comes from a just God who deals with sin but also delights to restore. The offer of peace to those far and near (verse 19) became the inspiration of the apostle Paul (Ephesians 2:17) where he saw Jew and Gentile both at peace with one another because they are at peace with God. This horizontal peace will never be found until there is the vertical peace between God and his people.

Sadly there will be those who will reject God's offer of peace; it can never be forced. In the Bible judgment is often seen in terms of salvation refused. The wicked who have no peace are paying the price of their rejection of the one who is the Prince of Peace (9:6).

Questions
1. There is a note of hopelessness in verse 10. How far is this true of society today and how are people reacting because of it?
2. Verse 15 describes God's special relationship with those who are broken. How far does it apply to your church and its spirit?
3. God's anger turns to acceptance. When you have righteous indignation are you also ready with the spirit of forgiveness? If not, how can it be cultivated?

Isaiah 58:1–14

Pure religion

True religion is not to be found in pious observances, such as fasting, but in caring for the oppressed.

 This chapter contains the classic voice of prophecy reminding us of Micah 6:8 and James 1:26 and 27. It is a call to love God and to love each other and to break with empty religious customs. But there are some external observances which must continue such as the keeping of the Sabbath as a mark of loyalty to God. Here love for neighbour and love for God are two sides of the same coin.

False religion   (verses 1–12)

The chapter begins with the voice of protest. There is a vehement, passionate shout in verse 1 against all spiritual rebellion and sins which continue even when the outward marks of obedience are found. All the right religious signs are there (verse 2) but there is no heart of obedience, no life of consistency. Isaiah speaks out against empty formalism here as he does throughout his book. There is no answered prayer (verse 3a) because God is not deceived by the outward show. In his practical letter, James highlights the reason behind unanswered prayer as wrong motivation and attitudes (James 4:1–3). The specific issue was one of fasting which continued and even extended during the time of the exile but often had no reality behind the outward show.

Jesus too referred to the danger of mere outward performance in fasting. His teaching is clear in Matthew 6:16–18, not denying the value of giving time to prayer through fasting but pointing out very pertinently the insidious dangers. Genuine penitence and faith are seen in terms of justice and caring love.

181

But alongside the voice of protest there is also a voice of promise. On God's conditions blessing will come as promised in Malachi 3:10. One condition is social reform, called for in verse 6, and another is the practical loving care for the needy (verse 7), a subject spoken of later by Jesus in Matthew 25 and relevant to us today. In these searching words there is the practical challenge to end all malicious talk (verse 9b). Then we can expect the promise of light and healing (verse 8), divine protection (verse 8b), and answered prayer (verse 9a). The metaphors pile up in verses 10–12, all on the theme of light and satisfaction. The picture of natural restoration in verse 12 is a word of hope in a day of tension and continued strife. With no great imagination we can see how verse 12 could be uplifting and encouraging to the broken world of today.

True faith   (verses 13–14)

The prophet reminds his readers of the importance of the Sabbath, not in legalistic but in loving terms. These words could well be used to Christians concerning their attitude to the Lord's Day.

Our love for the Lord is seen in loving our neighbour. Jesus challenged Peter to prove his love by his attitude to the flock (John 21). But we do also have a responsibility to the Lord personally. The promise of joy in the Lord (verse 14) and spiritual exaltation is linked with delight to be in the presence of the Lord and especially on the day he has set aside for worship.

If we claim to love the Lord we should then love his day. To the Jew the Sabbath was a part of God's original plan for everyone as well as an integral part of the law for the Israelites. It takes on a new dimension after the resurrection and moves from the last to the first day of the week. We find here a recipe for healthy living and also a mark of love and loyalty. Sabbath observance calls for an end to self-concern and self-pleasing. There is a note of duty and obligation in it which paradoxically brings pleasure, in the truest sense, to a person. There is a danger in neglecting being with God's people, and, possibly, failure to encourage each other (Hebrews 10:25). The Sabbath and the Lord's Day are both holy and yet a delight. Here we find strength and challenge not to escape the world but to re-enter it with renewed vision and vigour.

Questions

1. Beliefs and morals are always close to each other. In what way do these verses demonstrate this?
2. There is reference in these verses to unanswered prayer. Do we find that problem in the life of our church? How do we cope with it?
3. Fasting and Sabbath observance can become formal and legalistic. Looking at your own life, how do you treat these two marks of spirituality and allegiance to God?

Isaiah 59:1–21
Eden: action replay

The disobedience of his people causes God to turn away from them, but the prophecy is that Eden will be restored by the Redeemer.

 We are reminded now of the fall and the spiralling growth of sin recorded in the book of Genesis. What was in the beginning always is, in our world. Yet there is always a promise of divine intervention. The scene is set in verses 1 and 2 with God's presence in power and yet strangely also his absence because he recoils from our sin.

God turns away, disgusted   (verses 1–15a)

Sin always separates, as we see from the story in Genesis 3 when man and woman sought to hide from God and were eventually ejected from the garden. Yet in a way God hides from us because of our sin. The picture in these verses is of a very personal God, with references to his arm, his ear and his face (verses 1–2). His apparent deafness (verse 2) is because sin has come between us. If sin separates it also spreads and the mounting sin and anarchy of verses 3 and 4 was not only true of Isaiah's day, it has a very contemporary ring. In verses 5–6 it becomes a deadly poison until, in verse 7, murder is the norm and human life has become cheap. Paul quoted verses 7 and 8 in Romans 3:15–17 as he showed the universality of sin and the reality that all mankind is under the judgment of God. The price of this spiralling sin is that peace is lost in society (verse 8).

Sin also slays. The little word 'so' in verse 9 highlights the consequences that follow. Morality itself will disappear. One generation will get rid of biblical doctrine and the next generation but one has no time for morality. All the great values become victims. Verse 10

184

a grim reversal of chapter 58:10. In the previous chapter there is light at midnight; in this chapter there is darkness at midday. It is all the result of the sinful rebellion described in verses 12 and 13, as a result of which four great virtues are seen as fallen prostrate in the streets of Jerusalem (verse 14). By now the good person becomes victimized (verse 15), the only one to be out of step. This is a picture of perverted public opinion today as well as in Isaiah's time.

God returns to his people (verses 15b–21)

The renewal of hope is part of the picture, however, since all is not lost. God is concerned, and he acts through a solitary saviour. Here is the picture of a champion sent by God, a lonely warrior, to be seen again in chapter 63: 1–6. We can see Jesus in this picture, suffering profound loneliness, particularly in the Garden of Gethsemane and at the cross. The armour of God's warrior (verse 17) reminds us of Paul's teaching in Ephesians 6, and in verse 18 we are reminded that the cross is a picture of both God's love and of his justice. Ultimately, there is not only loneliness in the way of salvation but loneliness in the way of retribution.

Then in verse 19 the lonely figure merges into a crowded canvas. Jesus will be the second Adam leading many to new life (Romans 5:12 ff.). This is a picture of the world being won for Christ and it is promised by Jesus himself in Matthew 8: 10–12. What matters then is not race or religion but spiritual response and that will always include repentance (verse 20).

This repentance is our side of the New Covenant promised by Jeremiah and announced by Jesus in the Upper Room (Luke 22:20). One of the marks of that New Covenant would be the gift of the Holy Spirit to all who respond (*cf.* Numbers 11:29 and Joel 2:28). Heaven will, we hope, be a very crowded place but only because of the lonely faithfulness of our redeemer Jesus.

Questions

1. This chapter speaks of God 'hiding himself'. What does that mean and why does it happen? Is this why the world cannot see him?
2. Notice the theme of the loneliness of the Saviour in these verses. What message of hope does that bring to people in your church who are lonely?
3. Notice the four virtues mentioned in verse 14. How highly do these feature in your sense of priorities?

20

THE GLORY OF GOD'S CHOSEN PEOPLE
Isaiah 60:1 – 62:12

Isaiah 60:1–22

Blinded by light

A prophecy of the glory of Jerusalem; glorious because God's light will shine upon it.

Light is always a characteristic of the Christian gospel in contrast with the darkness of the world. So these verses can be seen as a preparation for the great prologue of John 1. In vivid poetry we see the dawn leaping over the horizon to be followed by the settled noontide of light. It speaks of the new Jerusalem after exile, the glory of the church and supremely prepares for us the picture of heaven.

A new dawn of glory   (verses 1–16)

Verse 1 uses feminine words in the original language and speaks of the city of Jerusalem awaiting her new dawn. This is not the earthly Jerusalem but the church of Jesus coming from Jerusalem which is above (in terms of Galatians 4:26). So these verses are true of the church today because of the ministry of Jesus (John 1:14). For Isaiah's generation there would no longer be a desolate Jerusalem but a city which would become the centre of a world movement, fulfilling its ministry to be a light to lighten the Gentiles (verses 3–4). In verses 4 and 5 we have the beautifully warm language of the radiance of motherhood.

But the growth of the church is as vital as the birth of the church. So we see a constant movement to Jerusalem overland (verses 6–7) and from overseas (verses 8–9). We are reminded of the story of the wise men bringing gold and other gifts to Jesus in the picture in verse 6 of bringing in the wealth of the nations. God's glory deserves the best offerings we can make.

Then in verses 10–16 there is the promise of final victory. Verse 11 has the note of a triumphal procession after battle and the same theme is used by Paul in relation to Christ in 2 Corinthians 2:14 (with himself included as one of the slaves in the procession). To reject God's kingship and ways is national suicide (verse 12), but there will be final victory for our Lord and his people with triumph over every enemy (verse 14). This is no foolish triumphalism to bolster up a troubled city. It is the sure finality of the defeat of all who oppose God and his ways. It will be seen in Satan's downfall, described in the book of Revelation (20:10).

The high noon of glory   (verses 17–22)

In whatever way we interpret these verses within the life of the church on earth, they also have echoes in the book of the Revelation referring to the fulfilment of heaven. In verses 17–18 there is the promise of full salvation with an end to violence and destruction. One day there will be a city whose only protection will be salvation and praise – its gates will be always open (verse 11). The kingdom of heaven is always marked by the qualities of peace and righteousness (verse 17).

Then in the closing verses comes the vivid picture of the new creation with its note of endless light. God's presence is all that is needed and in heaven he will be that light (Revelation 22:5). These verses remind us of other enemies that will be absent in the glory of heaven: no more sorrow (verse 20), no more sin (verse 21), no more failure (verse 22). These enemies are already being beaten back in the life of the believer, but will be fully defeated only in heaven. Scripture always has within it the note of 'now' and 'then'. That can be seen most pertinently in reading 1 Corinthians 13. We are foolish to imagine that we can enjoy everything now. Some things will remain for 'then'. So the apostle Paul could rejoice in the light that flooded his soul on the Damascus road when he was blinded by light (2 Corinthians 4:6), but he always looked on to the fulfilment of it in heaven.

Questions

1. Verse 12 talks about national suicide in rejecting God. Ponder what that means for your nation and turn it into prayer and action.

2. Here we have some vision of overseas mission and all nations gathered into the kingdom. How highly does overseas mission rate in your church?

3. Are you guilty in trying to bring into the 'now' those things that can only be 'then' and do you leave for 'then' what you could enjoy 'now'?

The city

As a city dweller Isaiah had a vision of the restored Jerusalem fading into the glorious image of heaven itself. This will be picked up in the language of the book of the Revelation (Revelation 21). But the phrases used in Scripture of that city to come demonstrate the difference between that and city life as we normally know it in the world of today.

Here in Isaiah 60:14 it is the city of the Lord where he is acknowledged and where he reigns. In 1:26 it is the faithful city, the city of righteousness. In 62:4 it is seen as the city married to God and therefore delightful. In Ezekiel 48:35, at the climax of that remarkable prophecy, the name of the city is 'THE LORD IS THERE'. In Zechariah 8:3 it is seen as 'the City of Truth' and the New Testament vision in Hebrews 12:22 is of 'the heavenly Jerusalem', the city of the living God. The aim of every city dweller of today should be prayerfully to make that the goal of the plans for city life here on earth.

Isaiah 61:1–11

Liberation

The 'year of the Lord's favour' denotes freedom for his people. What that means is explored in this chapter.

 This passage has a special significance because it provided the text of our Lord's famous sermon at Nazareth when he said quite clearly, 'Today this Scripture is fulfilled in your hearing' (Luke 4). He also quoted it in Luke 7:22 with a message to John the Baptist in prison. Jesus' use of these verses helps to warn us against interpreting them too literally. Their meaning may include a literal release from prison for some, but the basic message is that true liberation stems from the proclamation of the *good* news. This is a release of the spirit and mind rather than the body.

News of liberation (verses 1–4)

These verses give us God's manifesto with clear promises. The 'poor' refers particularly to the Jews in exile but the gospel will cross all barriers and involve the disadvantaged of every kind. The promise brings a word of comfort to the broken-hearted and a word to the captive. Sometimes God breaks down prison doors literally as in Acts 12 but more normally this liberation speaks of freedom from a greater slavery. It links with our Lord's words on freedom in John 8:31–36 and Paul's in Galatians 5:1.

All of this refers to the era of the Lord's grace. When Jesus preached he stopped short of referring to the day of vengeance, not because he did not believe in it but because that was yet to come. First there had to be the ministry of salvation through his life and death. But the day of vengeance is real (*cf.* Acts 17:31 and 2 Thessalonians 1:7–8).

191

God's manifesto promises are always kept (unlike those of many political parties). So the joy and festivity of verse 3 will overcome the disappointment and the faintness of spirit, but not all the blessings of the gospel come in an instant. There will be a patient reconstruction, expressed in the picture of the oaks being planted and the ancient ruins being rebuilt.

News of restoration   (verses 5–9)

In the restored Jerusalem the tables will be turned. All the people of God will be called priests of the Lord. Here we see the beginning of the idea of the 'priesthood of all believers' of which the New Testament speaks (cf. 1 Peter 2:5). There are many exciting pictures of the church here; the 'double portion' (verse 7), the everlasting covenant (verse 8) and a people whom the Lord has blessed (verse 9). The church's witness in the world should be exciting, not tedious and dull. Only then will the world come to acknowledge the supremacy of God, as depicted in verses 5 and 9. Roles will be reversed ultimately in the Kingdom of God.

News for exaltation   (verses 10–11)

As we have mentioned, the work of God's Spirit often leads to singing. Earlier in Isaiah's prophecy, chapter 12 is full of praise after the great truths of chapter 11. In verse 10 we find the joy of justification (see next page) described as the robe of righteousness. Jesus used the analogy in his parable of the wedding garment (Matthew 22:11) and it is the basis of the New Testament doctrine of justification. The beauty bestowed on the bride of Christ (his church) is all undeserved. It is a love-gift.

Verse 11 anticipates the doctrine of sanctification with its picture of the fruit of the Spirit as expounded in John 15:1–8 and Galatians 5:22–23. This is a gradual process but still all by God's grace. True liberation does not exclude a Christian concern for the hungry, the poor and the prisoner of conscience, but the heart of liberation is the gospel, the good news that Christ died and rose again to secure our forgiveness, freedom from sin.

Questions

1. Study how our Lord uses this passage in his sermon in Luke 4:14–30. How does this help in your understanding of it?
2. There are promises here of gospel ministry to the disadvantaged. Think of some of these in the life of your church.
3. There is a recurring picture of patient rebuilding and growth here. How far are you ready to be patient in waiting for the Lord?

Justification and sanctification

Justification is the apostle Paul's great theme. Of the thirty-nine occurrences of the word in the New Testament, twenty-nine come from the pen or lips of Paul. It was his great discovery that justification was by grace through faith and his life was transformed in the understanding of it. By background he was led to believe that he could earn his salvation; by experience he discovered that justification was a free gift of God and that he was accepted, not because of his merits, but because of Christ's merit. So Romans 5:1 became his passionate heartcry and, rediscovered by Martin Luther, was the great motto of the Reformation. It is a reminder that we are accepted once for all through Christ's atoning death and we are accepted in him. The classic example is the story of the penitent thief who, without any possibility of proving the truth of his faith in action, was accepted by Jesus because of his words of faith.

Paul was sometimes attacked because his doctrine of justification seemed to lead to a lax view of morality. In Romans 6 he disputes this argument and points out that those who have been justified should be deeply concerned to become 'sanctified', a process by which we are made holy and summed up by Paul in 2 Corinthians 3:18 as 'being transformed into his likeness'. Here in Isaiah 61:10 there is the picture of the garments of salvation with which we are clothed. This is the message of justification and at the same time a picture of the fruit of growing righteousness. This growth is the work of the Spirit in the lives of believers who have been accepted by God's grace and have accepted him by faith alone.

Isaiah 62:1–12

A wedding invitation

Jerusalem is seen as a bride and God himself is the bridegroom.

 The picture of marriage appears frequently throughout Scripture, leading up to the bridal feast of the Lamb in the book of the Revelation (Revelation 19:7). In the Old Testament we find it in the story of Hosea and it occurs frequently within the prophecy of Isaiah. The message behind this picture is a double 'I will'; both the people and God himself say 'yes' to Jerusalem.

God's offer   (verses 1–5)

The great yearning of the bridegroom is reflected in verse 1. He will offer a new name to his bride (verses 2, 4 and 12). The bride here is happy to exchange her old name for the new (*cf.* Psalm 45:10 and 16). Verse 4 contrasts the two names: now Jerusalem will be 'delight' (Hephzibah) rather than 'desolate'. In verse 12 there is a fourfold name of the new community, all reminding us of God's grace (*cf.* 1 Peter 2:9–10).

With this new name goes a new beauty of splendour and royalty (verse 3) and glory (verse 2). True love makes a person more attractive and the bride is delighted to be worthy of her calling (*cf.* Ephesians 5:27). In verse 5 we find a new joy. The wedding feast throughout Scripture depicts the joy of the bride being brought home. This is a very different picture from the erotic use of this illustration in Baal worship and many cults even of our day. There is purity, wholesomeness and reverence in the biblical picture. It fits with the whole concept of sex in the Bible; one man, one wife for life and no sexual intimacy outside that relationship. Without that, the Bible picture makes no sense at all (see Genesis 3:22–24).

Human effort   (verses 6–12)

In this section there is the responsive 'I will' of the bride. It is seen first of all in the prayers of the watchmen in verses 6 and 7. Here are people who 'call on the Lord', a phrase denoting worship, from Genesis 4:26 right through Scripture (*cf.* 1 Corinthians 1:2). Here are people who share God's concern for Jerusalem and whose prayers are part of his purpose and plan. Ultimately we never understand how prayer works. But we know it is part of God's ordering of events. Our prayers do matter.

The solemn oath of verse 8 leads to the promise of full enjoyment for the people of God in verse 9. Verse 11 reminds us of Palm Sunday, the triumphal arrival of the Lord.

But there is nothing automatic here. The whole section calls for action as well as prayer. So in verse 10 in urgent language we are called to go through the door (NIV – gates) and to open the door for others. Our Lord used that same language in John 10:9–10 referring to himself as the door (NIV – gate) into safety, liberty and true satisfaction. Behind all these analogies and pictures there is the theme of God's love calling for our responsive love.

Questions

1. Consider the meaning of the marriage picture as it relates to God and his people.
2. If we are called to be prayerful watchmen, what does that say about the priority of intercession in the life of your church? Your own life?
3. In terms of verse 10, how do you open the door for others to enter the Kingdom?

Baal worship

The Hebrew noun 'baal' means master or husband. But it became associated with the Baal worship in Canaan which all too often compromised Israelite religion in the Promised Land. 1 Kings 18 demonstrates the great moment of confrontation when Elijah summoned the prophets of Baal to the great contest where Jehovah finally triumphed. Baal was a name for many local gods, but was always linked with the idea of fertility and procreation. The worship made no demands for holiness but often the reverse. Baal had a consort called Ashtaroth and often it seems that we have had to introduce a goddess because of the insatiable desire of people to have a female sex symbol in religion.

So deeply was Israelite worship compromised, even merging worship with Jehovah with worship of Baal, that Hosea had to say that no more should they call Jehovah 'master', but he must be called 'my husband' (Hosea 2:16). The word 'master' was the word 'Baal' and all too often that name was the excuse for worship which did not fit the revelation of the true God who demands holiness and not mere ritual. He is the God who really does preside over the seasons and is providential over matters of life and death.

21

GOD: PRESENT AND ABSENT
Isaiah 63:1 – 64:12

Isaiah 63:1–19

A glimpse into the Godhead

God's day of vengeance is also his day of redemption. The work of the Spirit is reviewed in Israel's history.

 This is a moving and intense passage. Salvation is won but many are not willing to respond. For those who reject it there is solemn judgment. This section builds up to the end of the book with a mixture of welcome and rejection. Yet here we can also focus on God as Saviour, Father and Spirit, a glimpse of the full doctrine of the Trinity which we find in the New Testament.

The Saviour who brings salvation   (verses 1–6)

Loneliness is the key thought here. The solitary Saviour clearly foreshadows Jesus, a majestic picture of the one who comes 'mighty to save'. There is a hint of the second coming of Jesus in verse 1 but we are also focusing on his death. In the salvation he brings there is nothing cheap. There is a horrific picture of blood in verses 3 and 6 which is necessary as Jesus works out our salvation (verse 5). There can be no peace without bloodshed, no liberation without sacrifice (Hebrews 9:22).

There is a play on words in verse 1; Edom means red and Bozrah means grape gathering. A similar picture of blood-stained clothes and treading the wine press is used in Revelation where judgment upon God's great enemy will be fulfilled (Revelation 19:11–16). The final hour of the ministry of the Saviour would be both victory and judgment, a day of vengeance and a year of redemption (verse 4). We should never be ashamed of the centrality of the theme of blood in the gospel.

198

The Father who plans salvation   (verses 7–19)

The statement of verse 16 is repeated often in these chapters (*cf.* chapter 64:8). It expresses a longing for God the Father to show himself. The prayer starts with praise (verse 7) and with remembrance of the past, which is a good model for all who cry out of the depths. Equally important is the fact that this prayer is in the first person plural (verses 16–17), as was the great prayer of Daniel in exile. A prophet must be one with his people. He includes himself in the prayer.

He reminds God of his unique relationship with his own people in the intimate language of verse 8. The loving Father is always distressed at the rebellion of his children (*cf.* 1:2 and 4). Here in verse 9 the prophet returns to the theme of the Exodus. In the wilderness wanderings God still acted as Father (verse 12) but where there was rebellion judgment had to come and God even became their enemy (verse 10b). The heavenly Father will always chastise in love.

In verses 15–19 there is a call to God to act as Father with power balanced by love (verse 15). Sin has left its indelible mark in estrangement (verse 18) and a hardened heart (verse 17). Part of God's judgment is the withholding of his intervention (verse 15b). It is right to pray to God to return (verse 17) and to bring true revival (verse 19). A loving father delights to answer that kind of bold and sincere intercession.

The Spirit who applies salvation   (verses 10, 11 and 14)

There is no full doctrine of the Holy Spirit in the Old Testament. They were still awaiting Pentecost and the outpouring of the Spirit, but the Spirit of God was at work. In verse 11 he is seen as guiding his people and he is more significant than the angel of God's presence (verse 9). In verse 14 is the promise of rest in the Holy Spirit and a hint of the New Testament doctrine of the Comforter (NIV 'counsellor': John 14–16). But he is not a mindless power and there is the danger of grieving the Holy Spirit (verse 10), through rebellion, a theme of Paul's in Ephesians 4:30. Isaiah is anticipating the New Testament revelation of God in his three persons and our willingness to respond to his ministries and follow his way.

Questions

1. Consider the link between God's love and God's wrath as seen at Calvary and worship with gratitude.
2. Think of the picture of God as Father, Saviour and Spirit in these verses and ask how that affects your understanding of God.
3. What does it mean to grieve the Holy Spirit? Are you guilty of it?
4. Does the horrifying picture of God's vengeance help you to see the world in a clearer light? What difference does it make to your attitude?

The Trinity

This is the belief that God is one being, but within that One are three persons, Father, Son and Holy Spirit.

The word itself does not appears in the Bible and yet throughout Scripture the Trinity is assumed. It begins with the great affirmation of Deuteronomy 6:4 that God is one, and this is never denied. But even in Genesis 1 there is an awareness of the Persons of the Trinity working together in creation. God created, God said (the Word) and the Spirit moved. In the New Testament in Mark 1:9–11 at our Lord's Baptism there is the voice from heaven, the dove symbolizing the Spirit and Jesus offering himself in baptism. The angel, in announcing the coming of Jesus (Luke 1:35), speaks of the Trinity and Jesus, in his very clear teaching in the upper room (John 14) speaks of the ministries of Father, Son and Spirit together. Not surprisingly, his final word of the great commission involves baptism in the name of Father, Son and Spirit (Matthew 28:19–20).

The epistles are clearly based on this doctrine. The gifts of the Spirit in 1 Corinthians 12:4–6 are in fact the gifts of the Trinity. Peter introduces his letter with a clear statement of their integrated ministries in 1 Peter 1:2 and Paul ends 2 Corinthians 13 with the same theme. It is not a formula so much as an expression of the reality of the Christian experience. That experience is summed up well in Ephesians 2:18 where, in personal commitment and in continuing prayer, Christians come through Jesus to the Father in the Spirit.

The Holy Spirit

In Scripture the Hebrew word *ruach* occurs 78 times in the Old Testament and the Greek word *pneuma* 379 times in the New Testament. Both words speak of wind or breath and reflect the activity of God in the lives of individuals and his created world. He is seen as a person and not a thing in Scripture. Sadly for centuries the English translation spoke of the 'Holy Ghost' which gave a sinister and almost mythical view of the Spirit.

In the Old Testament the Spirit came upon people for special tasks and particularly on the charismatic leaders portrayed in the book of Judges. There are promises of a greater day as in Numbers 11:29–30 when Moses longs for the day when the Spirit will come upon all, in Ezekiel 36 and 37 with a promise of the Spirit coming to give new life to God's people after their return from exile and the promise of all people knowing the work of the Spirit in the prophecy of Joel, quoted by Peter on the day of Pentecost (see Joel 2:28–32).

Our Lord himself is seen as ministering in the Spirit from the very beginning (Luke 4:1, 14 and 18). He himself speaks of the need for rebirth by the Spirit when he speaks to Nicodemus (John 3), and Romans 8:9 assumes that there can be no genuine New Testament Christianity without the indwelling of the Holy Spirit.

In the ongoing teaching of the New Testament, filling out the preparatory truths of the Old Testament, the Spirit is seen as the one who enables Christians with power to live holy lives, who produces the fruit of the Spirit in individual Christians, who gives differing gifts to differing people for the good of the whole church and who produces a deep fellowship. The individual Christian is seen as a temple of the Holy Spirit (1 Corinthians 6:19) and the church is seen as the temple of God's Spirit (1 Corinthians 3:16). Just as at Pentecost the Spirit came like a sheet of flame dividing upon each individual Christian, so the Spirit lives in the believer, but also makes that believer a part of the community of the Spirit.

Isaiah 64:1–12

Waiting for God

Isaiah shares the common experience of God's apparent absence. Yet God is always at work, even when we cannot see him.

The key to this chapter is in verse 4 which speaks of a God who works as we wait. Sometimes he seems to be hidden (verse 7) because of our sin but he is always at work: he is never out of business (*cf.* John 5:17). His work is both in judgment and in revival.

In judgment

The marks of God's judgment are scattered throughout this chapter. There are, for example, the deserted cities like a wilderness (verse 10). Homes are in ruin (verse 11) and treasured hopes are dashed. But there are hidden marks of judgment also. The wrath of God is working against all sin (verse 5) and in verses 6 and 7 we are reminded that even righteous acts done with wrong motivation are seen in God's sight as filthy rags. One translation of part of verse 7 says you have 'delivered us into the hand of our iniquities' (RSV). That fits the New Testament explanation of God's activity described in Romans 1: 24, 26 and 28, 'God gave them over'. Left to ourselves we write our own sentences. God's judgment is hardly necessary. We have condemned ourselves.

Yet the hand at work is still the hand of our Father (verse 8). Because he is Father he is entitled to discipline and chasten us (see Hebrews 12:4–13). The picture here is of the potter, as it was in 45:9 and 10. He is fashioning his work even through suffering, and in the plan of God suffering can be a very powerful weapon in fashioning beauty. There is a positive purpose in these verses, which is to build a new city out of the ruins of the old. This purpose can be translated by us both personally and in the church.

In revival

This chapter is in fact the prayer continuing from chapter 63:7. Behind the prayer is the consciousness of God's sovereign power available always for his people (verses 3 and 4). God's power is seen at work on Mount Sinai and in his unique intervention at the Exodus. Remembrance of the past will always give hope for the future. God intervened in the Exodus when the people of God were desperate. 'Man's extremity is God's opportunity.'

Our part is to pray, and that prayer should begin with a prayer for forgiveness (see verses 8 and 9). We dare to pray that we might be treated as a Father's children depending upon his love. We may remind ourselves, and even him, of his promised blessings which are never deserved but only humbly claimed. Prayer will then move into a desire for something new and that lies behind the passion of the opening verses with its prayer for God to 'come down' again in reviving power. These are awesome pictures of God at work and they remind us of Revelation 8 when prayer is the agency by which fire and wind and earthquake come to the earth, and of the story of Elijah on Mount Carmel (1 Kings 18:16–40).

The chapter, however, ends with a question mark. God is always ready but will his people wait for him?

Questions

1. How do we see signs of God's wrath in the world of today?
2. When we pray for God to come down in reviving power, how do we expect that to happen in the life of our church?
3. This chapter is about praying with expectation. As you look at your prayer life, how much expectancy is there?

22

THE CHALLENGE TO RESPOND TO GOD'S CALL
Isaiah 65:1 – 66:24

Isaiah 65:1–16

The great divide

The great divide will no longer be between Jew and Gentile but between those who respond and those who fail to respond.

As the prophecy moves towards its end, Isaiah honestly records both glory and shame. Verses 13–16 contrast vividly: 'my servants ... but you'. Isaiah's message from the beginning was one of the remnant returning. Paul quoted the first two verses in an evangelistic note in Romans 10:20–21. Some will seek (verse 10) and some will forsake (verse 11).

The forsakers

The fact of rebellion appears in verses 1–7. The unrequited love of verse 2 reminds us of the dramatic and sad story of Hosea. It is the tragedy of a people going their own ways in open defiance of God's law, dabbling in the occult, delighting in evil, even proud of the sordid. The rebellion is especially seen in disobedience to God's revealed laws and defiance of God's rules concerning sacrifice (verses 3b and 7b). The Old Testament warns about dabbling in spiritism (*cf.* Deuteronomy 18:10–12) but the warning was ignored by these people (verse 4a) and in utter defiance they ate forbidden flesh (verse 4b). Ironically they thought of themselves as being specially holy (verse 5a). The crowning insult comes in verse 11 with the worship of Fortune and Destiny, pagan gods of good fortune and fate. With such activity the people of God can have no compromise (*cf.* 1 Corinthians 10:20–22).

There will be inevitable fruit of that rebellion (verses 11 and 12). God is not to be mocked and his judgment is seen in the contrasting refrain of verses 13–16. It is used in Revelation 22:11 with its reminder that we choose our own destiny by our response to God, his laws and his love.

The seekers

There is a lovely pastoral picture in verse 10 (*cf.* 55:6–7). The people concerned are responsive, like those described in verse 1. God takes the initiative before we seek him (in direct contrast with the obstinate people described in verse 2). Often in the New Testament the Gentiles would turn to Christ while the Jewish people turned their back on him. This is summarized in the story of the prodigal son who came home in repentance and the older brother who stayed at home, but in the spirit of rebellion (Luke 15).

In verses 8 and 10 the responsive people are seen as a remnant people, the good grapes in the cluster. The remnant will be salt and light, saving the whole nation from corruption. That is a principle of God's activity throughout history. The Valley of Achor (verse 10) where Achan was judged (Joshua 7:26) will become a place of rest and hope (*cf.* Hosea 2:15). God can bring beautiful things out of evil.

Then the people will be rewarded (verses 13–16). This is both a future and a present reality. Now it is possible to cross the divide from death to life but one day it will not be possible. It all depends upon the faithfulness of God who is called the God of truth (verse 16), literally 'the God of Amen' (*cf.* Revelation 3:14). He seeks us with unfailing love. If we seek him we shall both find him and be found by him. If we forsake him the consequences are grimly clear.

Questions

1. Notice the way in which judgment is expressed in these verses. How do we understand it in New Testament terms, in the light of the cross?
2. Evil religious practices are described in these verses. How can we be aware of them creeping into our church? What are they and how can we deal with them?
3. Note the promises of verses 13–16 and in your prayers claim them today.

Isaiah 65:17–25

All things new

A picture of the new heavens and a new earth.

 These verses prepare for the great promise of Jesus in Revelation 21:5 that he will make all things new. This prophecy has different dimensions. It speaks of the restored Jerusalem, it speaks of the church as a new Israel, and it looks on to heaven. There is something now and something not yet. It would be wrong to think primarily in terms of the Jewish nation, although the New Testament does encourage this expectation of God at work amongst his ancient people.

New Israel

The past is meant to be behind the people of God as they come back home. Zechariah had a vision in which he was reminded that it was not possible to build the new Jerusalem within the confines of the old (Zechariah 2). That is a spiritual principle which we must always remember. Tradition and continuity are important. Neither the world nor the gospel began with us. We need to value the way our faith has been handed down to us. But God is not locked into the history of the past. So in verse 17b there is a command to forget the past and Paul echoes that in Philippians 3:13. Spiritual progress depends upon knowing how to forget as well as how to remember.

For the present there are some gentle, undramatic offers but full of significance in the light of our Lord's offer of salvation and the work of the Holy Spirit. So in verses 18–19 there is joy in the Lord with the eternal dimension of verse 19b. This leads to the promise of a new and lasting life (verse 20) with the great note of constant renewal (*cf.* Isaiah 40:30–31 and Ephesians 4:23). With that there

208

comes the offer of security (verses 21 and 23), so different from the constant insecurity of Israel in the Promised Land (cf. 1 Peter 1:4). We need to beware of laying too much emphasis on treasure on earth. What matters most is fellowship with God (verses 23b and 24). This will be seen in a constant prayer relationship which proves how much we do belong to God and depend upon him.

Verse 25, however, speaks of the future with its heavenly promise. Ultimately, only in heaven will opposites be able to live together in perfect peace and reconciliation. But we are to make it our ideal on earth to live in fellowship with those who are not like ourselves and rejoice when we see it as happening within the body of Christ. Even so we pray that God's will may be done on earth as it is in heaven.

New Jerusalem

The reality always falls short of the ideal on earth but the vision needs to be maintained. One day sin will be destroyed and in verse 25 we look forward to the end of the serpent's ministry and his final defeat. Verse 20 gives us a picture of the assurance of eternal youthfulness. These promises can be seen as the reality of Eden restored (cf. Genesis 3:14–15 and Romans 16:20).

Salvation is also promised in these verses (see especially verse 17 and link it with 2 Peter 3:10–13 and Revelation 21:1–5). The promise looks on to the reality of the bridal day of the Lamb in the future and the end of all suffering and pain (verse 19b). This will happen in the final reign of the messianic King in the power of the Spirit. Verse 25 connects to the promise of peace in 11:6–9, yet another reminder of the unity of this remarkable book. Eden will be restored, creation redeemed, the wicked no longer flourishing and salvation enjoyed.

Questions
1. Consider from these verses what we may expect now and what still must be in the 'not yet'.
2. This chapter is not primarily speaking about the Jewish people today but it is a reminder that we should pray for them constantly. Are we guilty of forgetting this? How can we help them?
3. Forgetting the past is an important exercise in spirituality. How are you dealing with that?

Isaiah 66:1–24

A terrible ending

The prophecy of Isaiah ends on a mixed note of terrible judgment and a gleam of hope.

 No writer wants to end his book on a grim note, but Isaiah must be realistic. He has frequently spoken against the danger of dead formalism and warned of a sad division, and that note is sounded again here. Yet there are hidden gems, such as deep joy (verse 10), peace like a river (verse 12) and great security (verses 12b–13). But division always is present.

Division in worship   (verses 1–4)

The first two verses sound the great prophetic note. It was anticipated in 2 Samuel 7:6–7; 1 Kings 8:27 and Jeremiah 7:3–4. Stephen quoted these verses and paid the price in his martyrdom (Acts 7:49–50). Truth is often not very popular. There is no condemnation of the ritual of the temple itself here, indeed other prophets like Haggai would insist on the priority of building the temple. But Isaiah is rebuking all empty 'churchiness', dependence upon mere ritual and religious observance. You cannot put God in a box.

God delights in worship in the right spirit (verse 2b: cf. 57:15). True worshippers always tremble at God's word. The opposite of this attitude is seen in verse 3 where sacrifice is seen like a senseless slaughter if it is done without faith. Four legal sacrificial acts are contrasted with four unlawful sacrifices. The solemn judgment of verse 4 contrasts with the great promise of chapter 65:24.

Division in the family   (verses 5–14)

Family is important in Scripture but there are accounts and warnings of brotherly hatred in many places (for example, Cain and Abel; Genesis 4) and not least here (verse 5). Here is a warning of religious persecution. Verse 5 reflects a sad picture of religious life in many ages. Our Lord promised that we would be hated for his name (John 15:18–25). Judgment will have to begin at the house of God (verse 6).

The Father God is described with all the qualities of motherhood in verses 12–13 (see also verses 7–9 and Jesus' words in John 16:21–22). Isaiah uses the familiar Old Testament images of the temple (verse 6), the chariots (verse 20), the new moon and the Sabbath (verse 23), but he moves us on to the challenge of the end time. In the light of this, how important is the picture of security in verses 10–14. Yet even that ends with the solemn note of judgment on God's foes (verse 14b).

Division in eternity   (verses 15–24)

These words come very close to the words of our Lord in Matthew 7 where he speaks of two destinies. The way to heaven is the theme of verses 18–21 with the great picture of the people of God being gathered together for a final moment of victory. In the New Testament this is seen in terms of our Lord's return and the gathering together of the elect (cf. Romans 15:15–16). Then comes the promise of a new heaven and a new earth (verse 22) with God's glory at the centre (verse 18), and true worship continuing (verse 23).

Yet here too is the way to hell. The fire and the sword of verses 15 and 16 must be taken seriously (cf. 2 Thessalonians 1:7–10). There will be a special judgment on those who have sinned against the light (verse 17). The grim picture of verse 24 ends this remarkable book and is echoed by our Lord himself in Mark 9:48. Jewish synagogues have sometimes reversed the last two verses so as not to end on a grim note. But that is to amend God's word.

This royal prophecy is the story of God's amazing grace which we are free to accept or reject.

Questions

1. There is much here about division in the church. How far is that sad and how far can it be creative?
2. Isaiah objects to putting God in a box. How far is the worship of our church doing that?
3. With this final eternal division in view how are you motivated to go out with the gospel to reach lost mankind?

For further reading

Most commentaries on Isaiah are long and forbidding. For some Crossway Bible Guide readers who can cope with it the best and most recent commentary is:

Alec Motyer, *The Prophecy of Isaiah* (IVP, 1993).

The following articles in reference books will also be of great help:

Derek Kidner, 'Isaiah', *New Bible Commentary: 21st century edition* (IVP, 1994).

N.H. Ridderbos, 'Isaiah' and 'Isaiah, Book of', *New Bible Dictionary* (IVP, 1982).